Dedication

The City of London Freeman's Guide is dedicated to the memory of the many generations of my family who have lived and worked in the City, most especially to my father, David George Jagger, a Freeman of the City of London who became a Blue Badge Guide specialising in City, military and royal history after a full career in the Metropolitan Police during which he served in the Special Escort Group (SEG) and Royalty Protection.

Also, to my grandfather George Edward Jagger, who encouraged my interest in all aspects of City life. A proud Londoner, he lived and worked within sight of Bow Bells, carried the Finsbury Rifles regimental colour in the Lord Mayor's Show for many years and knew the City like the back of his hand.

Furthermore, to the memory of his father, resident of St Swithin's Lane, also George, who was so respected within the City that Police stopped traffic outside Mansion House to salute the passing of his funeral cortege.

A park bench dedicated to the memory of my grandparents, George and Maisie Jagger, may be found on the southern side of the gardens of Christ Church Greyfriars on Newgate Street. It is the ideal spot to sit for a lunch break while reading this book.

The City of London Freeman's Guide

Sixth or Sovereign's Edition published 2024

The right of Paul D Jagger to be identified as the author of this work has been asserted by him in accordance with the Copyright, Designs and Patents Act 1988.

www.cityandlivery.blogspot.co.uk

Cover design © Kura Carpenter
kuracarpenterdesign.blogspot.co.nz
Cover image of HM The King with the Lord Mayor © Gerald Sharp Photography

Printed by Short Run Press Limited, Exeter

This guide is also available in eBook format from Amazon, Apple and Payhip.com/cityandlivery

About the Author

Paul D Jagger is a Freeman of the City of London and Court Assistant of the Worshipful Company of Information Technologists - 100th Livery Company of the City of London.

He holds an MSc in Management from the University of Hertfordshire, is a Fellow of BCS The Chartered Institute for IT, a Chartered IT Professional a Chartered Management Consultant and Chartered Fellow of CIPD. He formerly served with 101 (City of London) Engineer Regiment (EOD). He lives in Hertfordshire with his wife and children.

Paul is on X, Instagram and Facebook as @CityandLivery

Also by the author:

> *City of London Secrets of the Square* Mile by Pavilion under the PITKIN imprint
>
> *The History of the Worshipful Company of Marketors*, privately published.
>
> *Songs and Music of the City of London*, privately published.

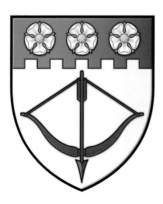

Sixth or Sovereign's Edition

This edition of *The City of London Freeman's Guide* celebrates the reign of King Charles III who is a Freeman of the City of London and a Liveryman of several of the City's companies, including his inherited status as a member of the Drapers' Company. In 2024 the Drapers' Company unveiled the first official portrait of His Majesty, continuing a long tradition of commissioning royal portraits.

This edition builds on the material in the previous five editions and incorporates all the updates that have been published in the eBook between print runs. The guide supported by the associated X account @cityandlivert, blog at cityandlivery.blogspot.co.uk and deep dive audio interviews with leaders of the City of London at cityandlivery.podbean.com

Author's Preface

Thence I proceeded on my way to London, that great and famous City, which may truly be said, like the Sea and the Gallows, to refuse none.

From an account of the life of Lot Cavenagh, tried for capital crimes at the Old Bailey in 1742

Every year around 1,900 people are admitted into the Freedom of the City of London. Each new Freeman is admitted in an ancient ceremony usually held in the Chamberlain's Court at Guildhall. Over half of those admitted into the Freedom are presented by one of the City of London Livery Companies, the bulk of the remainder being a combination of persons who are nominated for the Freedom or residents of the City wards. A small number are admitted as Honorary Freemen, and others take up a hereditary right to Freedom passed from either parent, in some cases through many generations.

Unique among the cities of the United Kingdom, the City of London still requires those standing for election to the local government of the City to be Freemen, a fundamental prerequisite for every elected office of trust in the City. Within the Livery Companies of the City of London it remains a requirement that members be admitted to the Freedom of the City of London before progressing to become Liverymen of their respective Companies. It is the Liverymen who in turn have the right to approve candidates for election to the office of Lord Mayor and directly elect the Sheriffs and certain other ancient officers of the City. Some 800 years after the first Freedoms were recorded, the Freedom continues to be both relevant and integral to the City of London.

Whether you are a prospective Freeman, a long-standing member of a Livery Company, or simply interested in the living history of the City of London, this guide highlights and signposts the wealth of available resources to enhance your understanding, appreciation and enjoyment of the City, Freedom and Livery.

As Doctor Johnson famously said:

When a man is tired of London, he is tired of life; for there is in London all that life can afford.

The London that Doctor Johnson spoke of was principally the City rather than the modern metropolis, a creature that started to grow to its current scale in Victorian times. There is more to discover among the resources outlined in this guide than you will likely have time for in your life, yet I hope you never tire of learning about the fascinating City of London.

NB. You may visit Dr Johnson's House at no. 17 Gough Square in Castle Barnard Ward.

What This Guide Is Not

This guide is not intended to be an exhaustive reference to all matters related to the City, Freedom and Livery. It is not possible to condense 2,000 years of City history into a manageable guide without necessarily leaving out much that might otherwise be mentioned. This is particularly true in respect of mentioning the history of every Livery Company, every ceremony, custom, office, event, institution and notable landmark in the City; some of those topics could easily fill an encyclopaedia. Nevertheless, I trust that the reader will find this guide a source of inspiration for further and deeper discovery in the areas of their particular interest. The history of the City of London has been exceptionally well documented, probably better than any other. Likewise, each Livery Company has its own history, much of it documented in rich detail. Inevitably this guide will forever be incomplete and out of date, as the tapestry of the City's living history continues to weave its unique and beguiling magic.

Acknowledgements

This guide would not have been possible without the support and contribution of all those who assisted in its development, review and publication.

First Edition

I would like to recognise in particular Mike Jenkins erstwhile Clerk to the Information Technologists' Company, for his encouragement and wise guidance in piloting this guide to formal endorsement by the Master and Wardens of the Company; Nigel Pullman, Chairman of the Livery Committee and Sheriff (2012-2013) for his sage advice and friendly critical review; Paul Herbage erstwhile Clerk to the Tax Advisers' Company; Tony Morrow, erstwhile Clerk to the Butchers' Company; and Jamie Wallis, Beadle to several City Companies, for their correction of many important points of fact; Sheldon Hind of the City of London Corporation for his advice on several aspects of the guide; Julian Cable and Stephen Plumb of the Musicians' Company, and Mrs Penny Boulet for conducting several rounds of much-needed editorial review; Christopher Histed of the Information Technologists' Company, for the inclusion of several photographs; and Kura Carpenter for the cover design; and finally the numerous prospective and recently admitted Freemen of the City of London on whom I foisted various drafts of this guide in order to test its popular reception.

Second Edition

The following City stalwarts further contributed to extensive review of the Second Edition: Mike Dudgeon (Mercer), Common Councilman Mark Wheatley (Draper), Alderman Alison Gowman (Glover), Chris Hodgkinson (Air Pilot), David Barrett (Clerk to the Makers of Playing Cards), Murray Craig (Chamberlain's Court), Nigel Pullman (Leatherseller), and Tony Sharp (Clerk to the Guildable Manor). I am further indebted to Tony Piedade (Information Technologist) and Julian Cable (Musician) for their contribution to the development of the Second Edition.

Third Edition

The following contributed materials, gave generously of their time and arranged private tours, interviews, or reviewed drafts of the Third Edition: Julian Cable (Musician), Kenneth Crawford (Merchant Taylor), Charles Henty (Secondary of London and Under Sheriff), Stephen Lane (Royal Society of St George), Kerri Mansfield (Information Technologist), Mike Paterson (London Historian), Stephen Plumb (Musician), and Nigel Pullman (Leatherseller).

Fourth Edition

Further thanks are due to Julian Cable (Musician), Nigel Pullman (Leatherseller), the Drapers' Company for the photograph of the portrait of Queen Elizabeth II that hangs in Drapers' Hall, to the Woolmen's Company for help with the cover image, Alan O'Connor Beadle to the Information Technologists' Company. Last but not least to my long-suffering and supportive wife who, despite working most of her life in the City, knew little of the City's governance or the Livery before we met but now knows more than enough about this subject of my endless fascination.

Fifth Edition

I am particularly indebted to the Drapers' Company, and its archivist Penny Fussell for arranging access to the cover image, also to the many leaders in the City who agreed to be interviewed for the Voices of the City podcast series that supports this guide.

Sixth Edition

The support of Fiona Adler, Secondary of London, Jo Mabbutt of the Livery Company Skills Council, Chris Fowler of the City Heritage Society, the Fan Makers' Company and Gerald Sharp Photography were vital to updating this edition.

Foreword

By the Right Honourable The Lord Mayor of London 2016-17, Alderman Sir Andrew Parmley

As 689th Lord Mayor of the City of London it gives me the greatest possible pleasure to write the Foreword to Paul Jagger's now indispensable *The City of London Freeman's Guide.*

Our ancient City develops every day. We have grown to become the unofficial capital of the world, the centre of global finance, a showpiece for culture and heritage.

But one thing has remained unchanged and at our core – the Freedom of the City of London. It remains one of the sources of our strength and our success.

Whilst all cities retain the right to confer the *Honorary Freedom*, it is only in the City of London that the Freedom is available to anyone, from any country, on condition they are of good character and have reached the age of eighteen.

The origins of the Freedom date from time immemorial; indeed, it is recorded as having been granted from the 13th century onwards. Thus, to be a Freeman of the City of London is to enjoy one of the oldest secular rights in the country.

To understand the Freedom it is essential to understand the City of London itself. The City, often called the Square Mile on account of its geographical size and shape, is run by the City of London Corporation, the oldest continuous metropolitan local authority in the world. The Corporation's two-house method of governance is the model for Westminster and its effectiveness has been admired over many centuries.

The prosperity of the City which brought Dick Whittington to London (or, at least, the pantomime version of him) was built on trade and this is where the Freedom became the key to a successful career. Indeed, in times past the cost of the Freedom was considerable and this accounts for the ceremony still being conducted by the Chamberlain of London, the Corporation's head of finance. In terms of trading, Freemen had valuable rights including exemption from certain tolls (probably the origin of the myth about herding sheep over London Bridge).

Today the Freedom may seem to be an anachronism, but nothing could be less true. The strength of the City and of its Livery Companies is derived from it; and the several Livery Companies in return adhere to the respected pillars of our civic lives – support of the City, charity, education, the armed forces and each Company's craft (or modern-day equivalent). Indeed, in terms of education the Livery is committed to providing high-class training, especially through apprenticeships, and what could be more historic and more relevant to contemporary thought than training and employability?

Paul Jagger's book is eminently readable and I commend it to you. Whether you read it from cover to cover or dip in and out reference-style – and whether you are the *youngest* (newly admitted) Freeman or an eminent Past Master – you are sure to learn something new.

The City, Freedom and Livery

Among the noble cities of the world which fame celebrates, the City of London, seat of the Monarchy of England, is the one which spreads its fame more widely, distributes its goods and merchandise further and holds its head higher.

William Fitzstephen, late 12th century

The City of London

The City is at least 2,000 years old, having been founded, or more likely enlarged and fortified, by the Romans circa AD43, then ransacked and burned to the ground by Boudicca and her Iceni horde around AD60, rebuilt and later abandoned by the Romans around the 5th century, and then re-established by King Alfred the Great in 886. The *sui generis* system of government operating in the City today has its roots in the Anglo-Saxon era.

The year after William I, Duke of Normandy, was crowned King in Westminster Abbey, he confirmed the ancient rights and privileges that the City enjoyed from Anglo-Saxon times in a Royal Charter that is still held at Guildhall. That document has been described as confirming the widest possible privileges in the fewest possible words and finishes by stating that the King would suffer nobody to do the City wrong.

The City is omitted from William's survey of his new kingdom as a result there is no mention of it in the Domesday book. This was no administrative oversight but rather a consequence of the influence of the City's merchants and the bargain they struck with the King.

Of the various clauses in Magna Carta, only three are still in effect, not having been repealed or superseded by newer legislation. Among them, Clause 13 guarantees *'The City of London shall have all its ancient liberties and free customs by land as well as by water'.* London is the only city mentioned by name in the charter. The City of London has a copy of Magna Carta and important as that document remains, from this City's perspective it only confirms rights that the City of London already held and exercised. We think about the City being an ancient institution in modern times; clearly it was considered ancient even in the early 13th century.

The oldest book written on common law is the *Liber Albus* or White Book of the City of London, a comprehensive guide to the laws, customs and offices of the City. It was written by John Carpenter, Clerk to the City in 1419 at the request of the then Lord Mayor Richard (Dick) Whittington, of pantomime fame.

If Westminster is the 'mother of parliaments' then Guildhall is, without doubt, the grandmother of parliamentary democracy. The true age of the City's unique system of government can never be known with certainty but it is likely to be at least as old as the High Court of Tynwald on the Isle of Man, which is recognised as the oldest continuous national parliament in the world. The City of London shares another characteristic with the Manx parliament - both legislatures are tricameral (comprising three chambers).

The City of London remains a visible and glorious anachronism, rife with anomalies that it is only too pleased to celebrate. The City retains many distinct characteristics that set it apart from all other cities in the Kingdom and it has always been a unique and special place with many of its rights and privileges existing by prescription.

The City is a ceremonial county, the smallest in the UK, yet it has no Lord Lieutenant or Deputy Lieutenants. The Lieutenancy is held in commission; the Sovereign's representative in the City is the Lord Mayor. The City is the only county that has two Sheriffs (but no High Sheriff), both elected by the Liverymen of the Livery Companies, rather than appointed by the Sovereign.

The City has its own police force and a panoply of civic and ceremonial officers not found in other cities, each adding to the pomp and circumstance of City ceremony. As a 19th century cartoon put it '*The City has many brightly coloured toys, and enjoys nothing more than to put them on display*'. The City is a place both within and apart from the boroughs of the metropolis - a sort of constitutional island that exercises immense power and discharges duties that have a positive impact on the nation as a whole.

The Freedom

The Freedom of the City of London is inextricably linked to the history of the City's governance and commercial development, the first recorded Freedom having been awarded in the mid-13th century. Originally a Freeman was one not bound to a feudal lord, able to earn wages, own and inherit (or pass on) land and property. Many supposed rights and privileges are associated with Freemen of the City of London, most of them apocryphal or long since lost in the mists of time, such as the right to carry a sword, the right to take a flock of geese down Cheapside, the right to be hanged with a silk rope, and possibly the most useful, the right to avoid arrest for being drunk and disorderly.

Copy of Freedom of the City of London belonging to the author. Although described as a 'copy', this is the original and only copy. The scarlet pouch can be used to hold the parchment1 certificate. Freemen who are also members of a Livery Company will be described on the certificate as Citizen & 'such-and-such', such as 'Baker' or 'Goldsmith'.

---

1 The parchment comes from the firm of William Cowley of Newport Pagnell, the last parchment and velum manufacturer in the UK.

Freemen of the City of London may be pleased to know that they are exempt from the community-based fine of Murdrum levied on the residents of any parish where a murder remained unsolved in early medieval times. Freemen are also exempt from the Press Gang, and from being subject to Trial by Combat. Furthermore, the Freedom is a hereditary right, inherited by children of Freemen so long as they were born after either of their parents was admitted into the Freedom. When sons and daughters of Freemen reach the age of 18, they may approach Guildhall to be admitted to the Freedom, and a long tradition exists of Livery Companies renewing their ranks with each family generation by right of patrimony. Sons and daughters of Freemen also have the right to petition the Court of Aldermen to 'translate' their Freedom to a Company other than that of their parents, a right exercised only a few times in recent centuries.

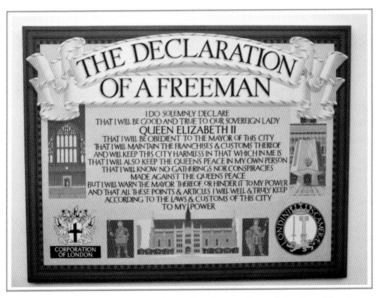

The declaration read by all those admitted to the Freedom of the City of London during a ceremony at Guildhall, now changed to reflect King Charles' reign. A slightly different version exists for persons who are not subjects of His Majesty.

Today the Freedom of the City of London remains a prerequisite for those wishing to stand for election in the City and is also a requirement for those Freemen (junior members) of City Livery Companies wishing to progress to become Liverymen (senior members) of their Company. Over half of those who are admitted to the Freedom do so by way of a Livery Company. Freemen of the City of London are entitled to take apprentices provided their deed of indenture is registered at Guildhall.

Freemen are also entitled to right of presentation for their children at certain schools, including the City of London Freemen's School in Ashtead, Surrey. Freemen who have fallen on hard times in old age, and widows and daughters of deceased Freemen, may apply to live in the City of London's Alms houses in Brixton. Widows of Freemen may additionally apply to the City of London Corporation for a small grant of money at Christmas. Freemen also have the right to join the City Livery Club, take apprentices (a legal process that is administered by the Chamberlain's Court in Guildhall), stay in the accommodation in either Vintners' Hall or Mercers' Hall, book themselves and their guests for lunch at the regular events held at a number of Livery halls, and participate in the annual sheep drive across London Bridge. Details of these and other events and activities available to Freemen are listed elsewhere in this guide.

The Lord Mayor, Aldermen and Citizens (Freemen) of London are mentioned in the proclamation of accession of the Sovereign in the United Kingdom, specifically as assisting the Lords Spiritual and Temporal in proclaiming the new king or queen. The proclamation is read by an officer of arms first at St James's Palace and then in the City where, by tradition, it is first laid before the Court of Aldermen for them to read.

Eminent persons of such wide-ranging renown as Dame Judi Dench, Stephen Fry, Alastair Cook, Placido Domingo and Sir Maurice Micklewhite Jr (not a lot of people know that) have also been granted the Freedom in recognition of their achievements, but these are not Honorary Freedoms despite what you may read elsewhere in the press and on the web.

On 13th July 2016, 'Citizen and Marketor' The Right Honourable Theresa May MP became the most recent Freeman of the City of London and Liveryman of a City of London Livery Company to be appointed Prime Minister of the United Kingdom. Past Prime Ministers who have been Freemen and Liverymen during Queen Elizabeth II's reign include Margaret Thatcher (Grocer, Poulter), Harold Wilson (Clockmaker), Harold Macmillan (Stationer), Clement Attlee (Ironmonger), and Sir Winston Churchill (Mercer). Some earlier Prime Ministers who were Freemen or Liverymen include Stanley Baldwin (Goldsmith), The Duke of Wellington (Merchant Taylor) and William Pitt (Grocer).

In times past, women were admitted to the Freedom as Free Sisters, although the word *Freeman* now applies to both genders, as does Journeyman, Liveryman, Yeoman, Common Councilman, Alderman, and the Lord Mayor.

The first admission to the Freedom conducted by means of web-conferencing software took place on 12 May 2020 when Captain [later Sir] Tom Moore was admitted by special nomination of the Lord Mayor. Captain Moore raised over £32m for the NHS during the Covid 19 pandemic while at the tender age of 100. Virtual admissions to the Freedom are now a routine option for those who cannot attend at Guildhall.

Captain Sir Tom Moore celebrating his admission to the Freedom of the City of London in the virtual presence of the Lord Mayor and Lady Mayoress

The Chamberlain of the City of London, Dr Peter Kane conducted the ceremony during which Captain Moore made the declaration and virtually signed the roll; the Clerk to the Chamberlain's Court, Murray Craig, spoke about the history of the Freedom and the rights of Freemen; the Lord Mayor congratulated Captain Moore on his admission and thanked him for his inspiring example to the nation. The following week Captain Moore was knighted by Queen Elizabeth II.

The event was broadcast live and a recording, with closed caption subtitles, may be found on the web.

King's Freemen

Following various Acts of Parliament, honourably discharged soldiers and sailors were once able obtain a certificate from the City Chamberlain exempting them from the requirement to be Freemen in order to conduct a trade in the City. This right existed from 1 April 1763 and continued into the early 19th century. Former soldiers and sailors who exercised this right were sometimes erroneously referred to as 'King's Freemen'.

The Honorary Freedom (*Honoris Causa*)

The Honorary Freedom is the City's highest award, and consequently it is rarely granted; indeed the book of Honorary Freemen has yet to enter its second volume. The first Honorary Freedom was conferred on William Pitt the Younger in 1757, and the first Honorary Freedom conferred on a woman was to Baroness Burdett-Coutts in 1872, the second was to Florence Nightingale in 1908.

The Honorary Freedom has been awarded to notable national figures such as the Duke of Wellington, Sir Winston Churchill, Florence Nightingale and Lord Robert Baden-Powell, and foreign statesmen such as Nelson Mandela, Franklin D. Roosevelt, Professor Stephen Hawking, and Desmond Tutu who received his Freedom not at the Guildhall as is usually the case but at Mansion House.

The Honorary Freedom is presented in a grand ceremony held at Guildhall and attended by the Lord Mayor, Aldermen, Common Councilmen and other City dignitaries, along with friends and family of the recipient. Before the award is made, a proposer and seconder are found from within the Court of Common Council, and a vote is held, to which the customary response is 'All'.

The recipient signs the book of Honorary Freemen and receives an illuminated parchment scroll that highlights their achievements. It is customary for the recipient to make an acceptance speech, and a reception usually follows, giving guests the opportunity to mingle.

The Honorary Freedom is in all other respects identical to Freedom by redemption, servitude or patrimony and confers the same rights and privileges.

In September 2014 the author was privileged to attend the Honorary Freedom ceremony for Sir Tim Berners-Lee, inventor of the World Wide Web. Sir Tim is also an Honorary Freeman of the Worshipful Company of Information Technologists.

Sir Tim Berners-Lee OM KBE receives the Honorary Freedom of the City of London from the City Chamberlain, overseen by the Lord Mayor, Aldermen and other City officials. Photograph courtesy of Christopher Histed.

Revocation of the Freedom

On 10 January 2019 the Court of Common Council voted to revoke the Honorary Freedom from the Burmese political leader Aung San Suu Kyi. This was the first revocation of the Honorary Freedom.

By extension the powers that permit the Court to revoke the Honorary Freedom also apply to regular Freedom admissions by servitude, redemption or patrimony.

Informal discussions by the author with the Clerk to the Chamberlain's court reveal that it is likely the regular Freedom has been revoked in the past, although little research has been done.

The City Obligation

The City Values Forum was formed during the Mayoralty of Sir Michael Bear (2010-11) to embed the principles of trust and integrity in the financial and business services sector and to improve business cultures and behaviours. The forum has developed a statement that succinctly captures the essence of what the City, and the individuals and organisations within it, should stand for. This statement is known as The City Obligation:

> *I will always treat others as I would wish to be treated, with honesty and integrity, in the spirit of the traditional City principle that 'My Word is my Bond'.*

This obligation is based on the motto of the London Stock Exchange 'Dictum Meum Pactum' (My Word is my Bond), wise words and a standard by which all Freemen should conduct their business.

The City's Livery Companies

The Livery Companies are a fascinating aspect of public life in the City of London ... nowhere is there such a concentration, nor can there be any set of private organisations which contribute so much to public life.

Professor Tim Connell

The Livery Companies are creatures unique to the City, the oldest among them being formed before the Norman Conquest. These early Guilds found their roots in the medieval religious fraternities of the City and soon adopted trade, craft or professional characteristics. In some ways the Livery Companies were precursors to modern professional bodies, trade associations or friendly societies, although they also had powers of search, inspection and punishment, and indeed some still do.

Livery Companies were granted wide-ranging powers and franchises through successive Royal Charters. The Company with the oldest extant Royal Charter, dated 1155, is the Weavers' Company, and they are also mentioned in the Exchequer's Pipe Roll further back in 1130. Note that many Companies style themselves 'the Worshipful Company of ...'., which recognises their religious fraternity origins – meaning that they are full of worshippers, not that they are deserving of being worshipped!

The Livery Companies grew in influence and importance such that in 1439 the Master and Wardens and Brethren and Sisters of the Guild or Fraternity of the Blessed Mary the Virgin of the Drapers of the City of London (a.k.a. the Drapers' Company) became the first corporate body to be granted armorial bearings (a coat of arms). This paved the way for every Oxbridge college, university, learned society and other corporate body that now has its own arms granted by the Crown.

The Livery Companies became involved in educating apprentices, regulating their trade, protecting consumers with early trading standards including inspection and enforcement, electing the Sheriffs and approving candidates for the office of Lord Mayor. They continue their role as an electoral body as part of the City's governance today. In modern times the Livery Companies continue to thrive and remain relevant, primarily as charitable and educational institutions, and contrary to widely held belief most still retain strong and substantive links with their profession, craft or trade. Some Companies still have substantial regulatory and inspection roles; the Goldsmiths and the Gunmakers are but two examples among many. Any preconceived idea that the Livery Companies are quaint and archaic relics with no modern role should be discarded. The Livery Companies are in rude health and most remain immensely active and influential in their respective spheres.

Arms of the Drapers' Company, granted in 1439 and the first to be granted to a body corporate. The Drapers' Company still has the original Letters Patent granting the arms on display in its hall.

The Livery Companies maintain a long tradition of fellowship evidenced by their formal dinners, shot through with ceremony and pageantry. One observer described the intermingling of charity and fine dining practised by the Livery as *'where philanthropy meets gastronomy'*.

In these times when casual dining is the norm, the Livery Companies retain the highest standards in formal dining with white tie, medals and decorations being the dress code for many occasions in the City (see Appendix B).

Robes, chains and insignia adorn the senior officers of the Livery Companies in a display of pageantry that is as diverse as it is visually striking.

This assiduous maintenance of tradition is done with a purpose. It fosters the timeless values of pride in belonging, high standards, continuity, and a sense of duty in the conduct of the Company's trade, craft or profession. No surprise then that serving and retired members of HM Armed Forces find a warm and familiar welcome among the ranks of the Livery.

But this fostering of tradition and high standards must not be allowed to eclipse the charitable and *pro-bono* activities of the Livery, which are exceptionally wide-ranging and substantial. Many of the more ancient Companies operate alms houses or other sheltered housing. By way of example the Skinners' Company provides sheltered housing in Palmers Green very close to where the author joined the Cub Scouts. The Mercers' Company is still administering funds left in the 15th century by one of its former members, 'The Charity of Sir Richard Whittington', albeit there is no evidence that Dick was never knighted: another quirk in City history.

Nurturing and reinterpreting ancient charities are not the only means of Livery Company philanthropy. The Companies are corporate bodies and use the profits from their businesses to fund a wide range of charitable enterprises. Many older Companies are blessed with properties and land donated by former members, but the younger Companies depend far more on the generosity of their current members either to fund their charitable initiatives themselves or to give of their time and expertise *pro bono* to honour their Company's charitable objectives.

A survey of Livery Companies in 2011 identified over 2,500 members actively involved in governance of charitable funds provided by the Livery. Over 450 members of Livery Companies are school governors and countless Freemen and Liverymen give their time, professional expertise and money to charitable endeavours in education, welfare, relief of poverty, the environment, arts and many other fields. It is estimated that the Livery donated almost 72 million pounds to charity and 110,000 hours of pro bono time in 2020, The value of the pro bono time and talent given by the Livery was estimated at a market value of a further 5 million pounds.

In 1515 (300 years after Magna Carta) the Court of Aldermen laid down the order of precedence that is still used today. Although it is not known what criteria they used to determine the order - probably the number of Lord Mayors fielded by each Company - certainly age was not the defining factor. Within this precedence, the first twelve in order form The Great Twelve Livery Companies, also sometimes known as the Twelve Great or simply the XII (and hereafter so described).

The annual exchange of gavels between the Skinners and Merchant Taylors, here overseen by the Lord Mayor, Alderman Vincent Keaveny CBE in 2022. Photo courtesy of the City of London Corporation.

Among the XII are two Companies who could not agree on their position in the order of precedence, resulting in a long-running argument which was settled by Lord Mayor Billesden in 1484 which required them to take turn. Since 1515 the Skinners and Merchant Taylors have alternated between position six and seven each year at Easter, possibly giving rise to the saying 'at sixes and sevens'. Five hundred years after Lord Mayor Billesden gave his judgement, the Skinners and Merchant Taylors published a booklet about the Billesden Award, a matter now settled: except that the Skinners and Merchant Taylors continue to disagree on how to spell that Lord Mayor's name!

Some Livery Companies have merged, such as the Armourers & Brasiers, the Painters and Stainers, the Barbers and Surgeons, the Stationers and Newspaper makers; some have split, such as the Apothecaries from Grocers, the Bowyers and Fletchers; a few have failed in the very distant past including the Bottlemakers,

Combmakers, Fishermen, Hatbandmakers, Longbowstringmakers, Pin Makers, Pursers, Silkmen, Silkthrowers, Soapmakers (a.k.a. Soap Boilers) and Starchmakers; and some have been absorbed, such as the Grey Tawyers (Squirrel skinners) who were absorbed into the Skinners, Hatters into the Feltmakers, Hurers (Cap makers) into the Haberdashers or the Gallouchemakers into the Pattenmakers. The Waterbearers seem to have washed away; the Woodmongers long fought with the Carmen, and much time was taken up in Parliament with the misdeeds of the Woodmongers. In 1667 the company had to surrender its Royal Charter but was reformed as the Fullers' Company in 1983. Since 2004 it has hosted a Woodmongers' Lunch with the Carmen to put old enmity to rest.

No new Livery Companies were formed between 1709 and 1926 and all those formed since 1926 are known as Modern Companies irrespective of the age of their associated trade, craft or profession. New Livery Companies join the order of precedence by the date they attain Livery status from the Court of Aldermen. Antiquity of profession is no indicator as to the age of the Livery Company as evidenced by the Worshipful Company of Educators, a Company that achieved Livery status in 2013, notwithstanding the fact that the University of Oxford grew out of a Guild of scholars more than 800 years ago; some might say that shows rapid progress in academia.

Although most Livery Companies are styled the Worshipful Company of such-and-such, anomalies and exceptions always exist where Livery Companies are concerned, such as the Honourable Company of Master Mariners and the Worshipful Society of Apothecaries. In 2014 the Honourable Company of Air Pilots re-styled themselves having previously been the Guild of Air Pilots and Air Navigators. The Air Pilots, like the Master Mariners, have royal patronage. In celebration of this renaming, HRH Prince Philip, Duke of Edinburgh, who was Patron of the Company, presented it with a magnificent ceremonial sword - just what every pilot needs in the cockpit!

Guilds and Companies without Livery

At the time of writing there are 111 City Livery Companies of which the Mercers are first in order of precedence and the Worshipful Company of Nurses is the most recent.

Currently (2024) there is one Guild in the process of seeking full Livery status: the Guild of Investment Managers. A Guild is the precursor to a City Company without Livery, which in turn is precursor to becoming a full Livery Company, following petition to the Court of Aldermen. There are also three City Companies without Livery: the Company of Communicators (formerly the Guild of Public Relations Practitioners) the Company of Entrepreneurs, and the Company of Human Resource Professionals.

Two notable Companies in the City are not Livery Companies but are recognised by the City: the Company of Watermen and Lightermen, and the Worshipful Company of Parish Clerks, neither of which intends seeking Livery status. The Watermen and Lightermen are the only City Company formed by Act of Parliament, and the Parish Clerks believe their white surplices are sufficient Livery.

These Guilds and Companies do not clothe Liverymen, hence they do not participate in the annual election of the Sheriffs or the Lord Mayor; neither do they have a position in the order of precedence.

There is also one religious Guild in the City, a survival from before the dissolution of the monasteries and the Reformation.

The Guild of St Bride, dating from at least the 14th century, finds its home in St Bride's Church. The Guild of St Bride once had a Guild House on the north side of Fleet Street.

Religious Guilds were probably the genesis of the occupational Guilds that evolved into Livery Companies, and as such the Guild of St Bride is a survival of that earlier era.

The Great Twelve

The XII are, in order of precedence, as follows:

1.   Mercers
2.   Grocers
3.   Drapers
4.   Fishmongers
5.   Goldsmiths
6.   Skinners / Merchant Taylors*
7.   Merchant Taylors / Skinners*
8.   Haberdashers
9.   Salters
10.   Ironmongers
11.   Vintners
12.   Clothworkers

*   These two companies alternate between positions six and seven every year unless the Lord Mayor is a member of either of these Companies, in which case his or her Company takes precedence.

Some handy mnemonics to remember the order of the XII are:

My Gracious Darling For Goodness Sake Make Haste Soon I'm Very Cold

Many Gross Drapers, Fish Golden Skins, Tailors Dash Salt and Iron Fine Clothes

In times past it was necessary for any Alderman who wished to become Lord Mayor to be a member of one of the XII. For those Aldermen who were not a member of one of the XII, a mechanism known as 'translation' allowed them to move their allegiance.

The heraldic banners of the XII Companies may be seen at Guildhall and below them the shields of the other Livery Companies including the most modern among them.

The Livery Committee

This body forms a vital link between the Livery Companies and the City of London Corporation. Founded in 1864, the committee was initially formed 'to consider the best means and take such measures as they deem advisable for securing the Guildhall from the intrusion of strangers at the meetings in Common Hall'.

In simple terms this meant ensuring that only those eligible to participate in the election of the Lord Mayor, Sheriffs and certain other ancient officers be admitted to Common Hall.

The role of the committee in modern times is two-fold:

1.   To oversee the arrangements for Common Hall at the Election of Sheriffs on Midsummer Day (24th June*) and the Election of the Lord Mayor each Michaelmas Day (29th September*).

2.   To act as the conduit for communication between the Livery (including its Masters, Prime Wardens, Upper Bailiff, Courts, Liverymen and Clerks) and the 'powers that be' at Guildhall (including the Chamberlain's Court), Mansion House, and the Old Bailey, on any matter affecting the interests of the general body of the Livery.

*   Or the nearest weekday thereafter.

The Livery Committee consists of representatives from the Court of Common Council (the City's governance body), the Livery Companies and the three Clerks' Associations (see City Clubs, Societies and Associations).

The Livery Committee operates a Livery Companies Liaison Scheme whereby each elected member of the Committee acts as a point of contact for a number of Livery Companies, principally to provide advice and guidance on Civic matters to the Master and Clerk of each Livery Company.

The closeness of the relationship between the Livery Companies and Guildhall is evident in the fact that all Aldermen and most Common Councilmen are Liverymen of one or more Companies. Guildhall provides extensive support to the Livery Committee and is the venue for many Livery Company social and philanthropic events. Conversely members of the Livery support the Corporation and Mansion House in various ways, not least by serving as external members on committees or assisting in the delivery of City Briefings. This relationship is, like so much else in the City, unique among local authorities in the UK.

Livery Company Associations

Several inter-Livery groups bring together the otherwise independent Livery Companies to coordinate their efforts in common cause.

One such group is the Financial Services Group of Livery Companies, founded in 2008, and composed of the following Livery Companies: Solicitors, Chartered Accountants, Chartered Secretaries, Chartered Surveyors, Marketors, Actuaries, Insurers, Arbitrators, Information Technologists, World Traders, Management Consultants, International Bankers and Tax Advisers. At the time of writing the Guild of Investment Managers has observer status within this group.

Other associations include one representing the leather trades, one for the metal bashers, and another representing users and suppliers of water known as 'The Wet 10' which in typical Livery Company style has a membership of thirteen. There is talk of forming a Binary Group of Livery Companies (those with following orders of precedence in decimal: 1, 10, 11, 100, 101, 110, 111) which would combine three of the XII with four of the most modern Companies, whereby the ancient can learn from the modern and vice versa.

Livery Company Links with Trade, Craft and Professional Bodies

In addition to the work that the Livery Companies do in direct support of their occupations (e.g., that Farriers, Goldsmiths, Gunmakers and Fishmongers all exercise powers over the trade), they maintain an immense array of connections with third-party trade associations, learned societies and professional bodies. In some cases, Livery Companies have corporate members or have partnered with businesses to further their trade.

The links are particularly strong among the modern Companies, such as the Information Technologists, which counts among its Liverymen many Past Presidents of BCS, The Chartered Institute for IT (formerly the British Computer Society), and the City of London Solicitors' Company which is closely connected with the Law Society's branch in the City. The Saddlers' Company provides support to the Society of Master Saddlers, and the Chartered Surveyors' Company and the Chartered Accountants' Company are both linked with their eponymous professional bodies.

The Brewers' Company has developed trade links to the extent that nearly 50 corporate members constitute the backbone of the Company. The Butchers' Company is, perhaps unsurprisingly, close to its trade in both geographical proximity (it is based in Smithfield) and in professional links with the Institute of Meat and the Meat Training Council.

Livery Company Connections with Freemasonry

The Livery Companies and Freemasonry are separate organisations that some historians believe share a common ancestry. One theory is that Freemasonry grew out of the Livery Companies in the late 17th century, although the evidence to support this theory is limited and circumstantial. One apparent link is that the United Grand Lodge of England has a coat of arms based loosely on the arms of the Worshipful Company of

Masons. Other parallels exist between Freemasonry and the Livery, especially in respect of their charitable endeavours and spirit of fellowship, but further comparison would be speculative since Freemasonry has spread globally whereas the Livery Companies exist only in the City.

In modern times, the links between the Livery Companies and Freemasonry are at the level of individual membership, rather than any formal organisational connection. That said, approximately one quarter of the Livery Companies have an associated Masonic Lodge, some meeting in the associated Company's hall; a list of them may be read in Appendix A.

Livery Company Halls

Of all the Livery Companies, ancient and modern, more than 40 have their own Livery hall, albeit that one former hall is a ship, HQS Wellington, which has a single anchor inside the City limits.

Some Livery Halls were destroyed in the Great Fire of 1666, while others succumbed to the Blitz, but the Cooks have been particularly unlucky, as their hall survived the Great Fire but was subsequently damaged by several fires, the last in 1771.

The Gunmakers' Company has premises known as Proof House outside the City on Commercial Road, apparently because the City authorities didn't want the noise of guns being tested in the City. This is one of two such establishments in the UK for testing small arms; the other is in Birmingham.

The Glaziers' Hall has one side against the southern end of London Bridge and hence within the City boundary but most of it is in Southwark. It is home for three Companies: the Glaziers, Launderers, and Scientific Instrument Makers, who have shared ownership.

Many of the Livery Companies that do not own a hall either lease offices or have arrangements with those Livery Companies that do own a hall. Examples include the Scriveners, who are based at IT Hall; the Paviors, who lease office space in Charterhouse; and the Fan Makers and others, who have their own offices adjacent to Skinners' Hall, with the right to use that hall for dining on certain days of the year. Others prefer to remain independent and enjoy dining in a wide variety of halls.

The Worshipful Company of Chartered Accountants has use of storage space in Chartered Accountants' Hall, which is owned by the Institute of Chartered Accountants in England and Wales (ICAEW). Until recently, the Worshipful Company of Insurers had facilities in Insurance Hall, which was owned by the Chartered Insurance Institute (CII). Neither of these are Livery halls.

The Masons' Company used to have a hall on Masons' Lane (now Masons' Avenue) in the City.

The Livery Hall of the Armourers' Company: a visual feast of heraldry, arms and armour.

The Girdlers' Company Hall surrounded by modern office blocks on Basinghall Avenue. Since 1933 the Girdlers' Company has hosted the New Zealand Society (UK) in their hall on Waitangi Day.

The Stationers' Company Hall being prepared for a Livery Company banquet.
Photograph courtesy of Christopher Histed.

A Livery Company Hall is a curious mix of a working office and a setting for the Company's various social events. Many of the Companies hire out their halls for both Livery and non-Livery social and business functions. Some of those halls provide a setting that is comparable with the most comfortably appointed stately homes in the country.

The Livery Company Halls are private property and not open to the public in the general sense; however, some of them may be viewed during the Open House weekend in September (see Places to Visit in the City). The Goldsmiths' Company opens its hall on certain days during the year, and tickets are available from the City Information Centre. The Armourers' Hall has recently entered the guided tours business and the author can confirm they are superb!

Several Companies provide a 3D virtual tour of their hall on their website; examples include the Goldsmiths' Hall, Saddlers' Hall, Stationers' Hall and the Plaisterers' Hall. Several virtual video tours of Livery Halls are also available on the internet. The author has identified the best among them in a YouTube channel; for details see the "Online Resources" chapter.

Navigation layout for the 3D virtual tour of Saddlers' Hall, one of several halls to provide extensive augmented reality tours.

On a more practical level, the addresses of the various Livery Company Halls, and former Livery Halls, are given in Appendix G and the author has produced a map as an A2 poster available in print and digital forms.

Livery Company Governance

*For over nine centuries the City has led the civilised
world in administration, justice, trade and finance,
fraternity, education and charity, in a unique pageant of
initiative and enterprise. Nowhere in the world has there
been such a concentration of excellence in so many
spheres. And much of this stems from the Livery
Companies and Guilds.*

Valerie Hope, *The Freedom 1982*

The precise governance structure of each Livery Company differs
somewhat from one to the next; the Companies have evolved at
different times with no overarching authority responsible for
governance of all Companies. The Companies are therefore
characterised by a bewildering range of differences in the titles
and composition of their court members (management board).

To this day, each of the Livery Companies is a fief unto its own,
clean and apart from the others. The Companies guard their
independence, customs and traditions jealously. Talk of a Livery
Movement is wishful thinking as the Companies maintain a
friendly and competitive rivalry. The only rule that binds
together every Livery Company is the rule of exceptions, of which
there are myriad!

In 1364 an ordinance of the Court of Aldermen stipulated that
*'all misteries of the City be lawfully ruled and governed, each in
its kind by good men elected and sworn from each mistery, so
that no deceit or false work be found therein'.* The word *mistery*
comes from the Latin *misterium* or *ministerium,* meaning a
trade or occupation. The Court of Aldermen at Guildhall still
retains the right to grant and approve amendments to a Livery
Company's charter, and no new Livery Company may be formed
without the authority of the Lord Mayor and Aldermen. It is also
to the Court of Aldermen that the Livery Companies would turn
in the event of a dispute among two or more Companies.

The heraldic banner of the Mercers' Company, seen here hanging at Guildhall. The Mercers are first in order of precedence among the Livery Companies.

The Master (or Prime Warden / Upper Bailiff)

An elected officer, usually known as the Master, heads each City Livery Company. The Master may be considered as the most senior Liveryman of the Company during his or her term in office. However, a Master is outranked in order of internal Company precedence by a Grand Master in the case of the Air Pilots, a Company Admiral in the case of the Master Mariners, or by a Permanent Master in the case of the Shipwrights, these offices each being held by a member of the Royal Family.

The Master is known as a Prime Warden in the case of the Basketmakers, Blacksmiths, Dyers, Fishmongers, Goldsmiths, Shipwrights (who confusingly also refer to their Prime Warden as Master), and now also the Saddlers - but only since 2015 when HRH The Princess Royal became the Saddlers' Company's third Perpetual Master in its 1000 year history.

Unique among the Livery Companies, the Weavers has an Upper Bailiff, and the Cooks find that having two Masters at the same time is curiously not 'too many Cooks'. The latter practice is derived from an incident in their history when the Master of the Cooks' Company was ordered to be present at both the King's banquet and the Lord Mayor's banquet simultaneously; a second Master was promptly elected to overcome the problem.

The Master, Prime Warden or Upper Bailiff is elected annually, with the exception of the Bowyers, who elect a Master to serve two years[2]. During their term of office, the Master, Prime Warden or Upper Bailiff should always be addressed as such, especially at formal or public events. A scurrilous rumour exists that past Prime Wardens of the Fishmongers' Company are informally described as being 'past their prime', but this cannot be verified.

The Master of a City of London Livery Company is so titled irrespective of the sex of the incumbent, although it has been said that a male Master's wife is described as the Master's 'mistress' because she invariably receives better treatment when so called! In the event that the Master's partner is male, he is usually referred to as a 'consort'.

Masters of Livery Companies are eligible to petition for a grant of arms if they are not already *armigerous*. Many Livery halls are richly adorned with the coats of arms of Past Masters, and where a Master has served as Lord Mayor, they are usually shown some special distinction such as having their heraldic banner on display in the hall, perhaps or on a stained-glass window. During their term of office, a Master will receive invitations to a wide range of social events and host many guests at events organised by their Company.

Past Masters

At the end of the Masters term of office he or she becomes a Past Master, and for the first year after their mastership they will usually be styled Deputy Master (immediate Past Master). The Deputy Master stands in for the Master in the event that he or

---

[2] The custom of electing a Master for two years was also observed by several other Livery Companies in times past. The Wax Chandlers changed to a single year mastership in 1978, and the Woolmen in 1932, and prior to 1839 that company's Master served a three-year term. One Past Master of the Horners' Company managed to serve from 1814 to 1840.

she is indispose. Most Livery Companies keep their Past Masters on Court for a number of years to ensure a wealth of wisdom is retained in the Company's governing board.

The Wardens

Supporting the Master are the Wardens, typical varying between two and four in number and usually holding titles in order of seniority such as the Senior and Junior Warden, although the Vintner and the Dyers both have a Swan Warden and numerous Companies have Renter Wardens and sundry other titles such as Free, or Foreign Warden.

In the normal course of events, the most senior warden would expect to progress to become Master, except in the case of the Coopers, where both the Upper and Under Wardens are elected by a group of Liverymen of the Company known as the Society of the Livery, and these Wardens are not in direct line to become Master. Some of the older Companies confusingly send their Past Masters round to become Wardens again, but do not usually progress to the chair again.

The Court of Assistants

The Master and Wardens, along with a number of Assistants, form the Company's governing board, which is known as the Court of Assistants (or simply the Court). Only Liverymen of the Company are eligible for appointment to the Court. The Court often delegates detailed governance responsibilities to various sub-committees, so as to reflect the diversity and scope of the Company's responsibilities.

The Liverymen

Liverymen are senior members of the Company who have the right to participate in the election of Sheriffs, Ales Conners,

Bridge Masters, City Auditors and the right of approval of candidates for the office of Lord Mayor, but only after they have been a Liveryman for a year. Liverymen also have the right to stand for election as a Sheriff and certain other ancient offices in the City. Some Companies restrict certain social events to Liverymen, with or without guests.

Many Companies have a limit to the number of Liverymen they may *clothe* (promote from Freemen), and typically 300 is the ceiling now imposed by the Court of Aldermen on modern Companies. A Company that has reached the limit of its Livery may petition the Court of Aldermen for an increase, usually in increments of 50, but they must present a good reason for the increase and it is by no means guaranteed the increase will be granted. Some older Companies are free to clothe as many Liverymen as they wish.

The requirements to become a Liveryman are entirely a matter for each Company and vary from one to another, usually a combination of seniority, contribution to the life of the Company, peer recognition, active involvement in Company events, eminence in their field and good behaviour. Rumour has it that fines for errant Freemen and Liverymen start with a good bottle of port and work their way up. Progression to the Company's Court is a clear indication that one has been judged to be *un très bon oeuf*.

The Freemen

Ranking below the Liverymen are Freemen of the Company, unless they happen to be Freemen of the Air Pilots' Company with five or more years' flying experience, in which case they are known as Upper Freemen but still rank below the Livery.

The Yeomen

To complicate matters even further, the Basketmakers, Upholders and Arbitrators have a grade of membership known as Yeoman, meaning a Freeman of the Company who has subsequently taken the Freedom of the City whilst in the Company. Other Companies use the term Yeoman differently, such as the Saddlers, who confer it on 'distinguished users of the Saddle', and the Musicians, who confer the title Yeomen on Company prize winners for a period of five years during which they receive financial support, mentoring and training, and benefit from raising their profile in the performing arts world. Some Companies also operate a corporate, affiliate or friends' membership status in various forms.

Livery Companies may also award honorary Freedom or Liveryman status. Some Livery Companies also have Royal Patrons. Some only admit persons holding relevant professional qualifications such as the Solicitors, Engineers, Chartered Accountants, Chartered Surveyors, Chartered Secretaries and Administrators, Insurers, and Tax Advisers, among others. The Brewers admit only directors and senior management within the brewery trade.

Modern Livery Companies are required by the Court of Aldermen to find the majority of their membership from those working in the trade, craft or profession represented by the Company, and as such are often described as a 'working Companies'. Modern Livery Companies will therefore usually require prospective members to show evidence of qualification, experience and achievement in the relevant trade, craft or profession. Some Companies will admit only members who hold Chartered status in their respective profession or similar 'licence to practise' qualifications. Most Companies will also admit persons who work in academic or scientific research or teaching allied to their trade.

Some ancient Companies have found renewed relevance by aligning with a modern industry in some way linked to their ancient craft. A good example is the Tallow Chandlers now supporting the Federation of Oils, Seeds and Fats Association, a body representing trades that use tallow in their industrial processes. The Horners' Company has allied itself with the plastics industry.

Together the Master, Wardens, Assistants, Liverymen and Freemen form the membership of the Company. The Company will also have a number of employees; most senior among them is the Clerk.

NB. Titles in the City are gender neutral. Men and women have been admitted to the Freedom for many centuries. All Livery Companies are open to men and women on equal terms and there is a substantial, and growing, cohort of female Past Masters.

The Clerk

The day-to-day management of a Company is entrusted to a Clerk, who is the senior salaried employee, a role akin to either a modern Chief Executive Officer or a General Manager.

Notwithstanding their title, Clerks to City Livery Companies should never be thought of as administrative pen-pushers. Indeed, the effective and efficient management of the entire Company rests principally on the Clerk's shoulders. Many Livery Companies employ barristers-at-law or retired officers of HM Armed Forces, some having reached the most senior ranks.

Livery Company Clerks are often referred to in one of the following ways:

- The Honourable Clerk to the Company of ... if a Barrister-at-Law, or
- The Gallant Clerk to the Company of ... if a retired officer of HM Armed Forces (as many are), or

- The Learned Clerk to the Company of … if holding a degree (as most will)
- The Gallant and Learned Clerk to the Company of … if both the previous two conditions apply
- The Worthy Clerk if none of the above apply

The Clerk will usually have a staff, the size and composition of which depends on many factors, including whether the Company has a hall to maintain, the number of members in the Company, and the range of charitable, educational and occupational activities the Company undertakes. Some Clerks benefit from an apartment in their Company's Livery Hall.

The Chaplain

The oldest Livery Companies find their origins in medieval religious guilds. Today Livery Companies admit persons of any faith or none, but every Company maintains a link with the established Church. The Chaplain to a Livery Company is an honorary appointment and is usually but not always an Anglican Priest who may also be Rector, Vicar or Priest-in-Charge of a Church in the City of London. The membership of a Livery Company are the Chaplain's parishioners (irrespective of faith). The Chaplain performs ceremonial, advisory and pastoral role in the life of a Livery Company.

The Livery Company Beadle performs many roles, including that of Master of Ceremonies, keeper of the Company's treasures and occasionally disciplinarian. An avuncular disposition and affable character are essential qualities.

The Beadle

Most Companies employ a Beadle on either a part-time basis to act as a Master of Ceremonies for formal events, or perhaps on a full-time basis if the Company owns a hall. In the latter case, their ceremonial role is often combined with that of a Hall Manager, responsible for running the Company's hall, especially if it is hired out on a commercial basis for weddings, parties and corporate events.

Traditionally the Beadle was responsible for keeping order in the Company, particularly among apprentices, and so carries a staff of office in procession (often erroneously referred to as a 'mace'). The Beadle's role is similar to that of a Verger in a Church and probably grew out of the religious guilds. It should be noted that the Verger of St Paul's Cathedral wears a robe of almost identical design to that of a Livery Company Beadle.

The Beadle is also charged with the safekeeping of the Company's possessions, especially the treasures. Many Livery

Companies employ retired warrant officers, senior non-commissioned officers of HM Armed Forces or retired police officers in this vital role. There is a long tradition of Yeoman Warders (Beefeaters) being employed as Livery Company Beadles.

Other Livery Company Employees

Depending on the size, wealth, age and range of activities performed by the Company, it may employ an archivist, a historian, a doorkeeper, charity administrative staff, event managers, a chef, catering staff and many other roles.

Officers of the City

Right Honourable Patron, to your state,
In duty I these triumphs dedicate.
For no King's deputy or magistrate,
Is with such pompous state inaugurate.
As London's Mayor is, which plainly shows,
The King's illustrious greatness whence it flows.

John Taylor, *The Triumphs of Fame and Honour*, 1634

The Right Honourable the Lord Mayor (of the City) of London

The Lord Mayor is head of the City of London Corporation and in the City ranks second only to the Sovereign, a fact confirmed by George III when his son the Prince of Wales argued over order of precedence with the Lord Mayor, and the King favoured the Lord Mayor over his eldest son.

The office of Lord Mayor dates from 1189. Originally simply the Mayor of London, the title Lord Mayor came into use from 1354. The first recorded Mayor of London was Henry FitzAilwin de Londenestone, a Draper who served 24 terms (years) in office. The office grew rapidly in importance such that in 1215 when Magna Carta was sealed, various Barons, Bishops and Abbots and one commoner were party to it. That commoner was a gentleman by the name of William Hardel, Mayor of the City of London.

A Lord Mayor must be a Freeman of the City of London and an Alderman. The Lord Mayor must also have served as a Sheriff and not previously served as Lord Mayor. However in April 2020 the Court of Common Council announced that Alderman William Russell would serve a second, contiguous, term of office as a result of the disruption to national life bought about by the Covid-19 pandemic. This was the first time since 1885 that a

Lord Mayor served two terms of office and the first time since 1862 that the Lord Mayor served two contiguous terms. This exception does not change the established custom that Lord Mayors should serve one term only.

At the time of writing, there have been two female Lord Mayors: Dame Mary Donaldson later Lady Donaldson of Lymington (Lord Mayor 1983-84) and Dame Fiona Woolf (Lord Mayor 2013-14). During her year in office, Lord Mayor Donaldson fined anyone who addressed her as Lady Mayor(ess) one pound, which was donated to the NSPCC. (The correct use of the term "Lady Mayoress" is to refer to the wife of a Lord Mayor.)

The Lord Mayor holds numerous other offices, inter alia: Admiral of the Port of London, Rector of City University London, Vice-President of Birkbeck College, President of the City of London Reserve Forces and Cadets Association, Governor of the Honourable Artillery Company, Registrar of Pawns, Keeper of the Great Beam, Gauger of Merchandise, Patron of the City Livery Club, Escheator of the City and Borough of Southwark, Clerk of the City Markets, Chief Magistrate of the City, Trustee of St Paul's Cathedral, Honorary Trustee of the Trealor Trust, Head of the Commission of Lieutenancy, Member of the Accession Council, President of Gresham College, Patron of the United Wards' Club and of the Guild of Freemen of the City of London, and perhaps surprisingly, President of the City of London Bowling Club.

During their year in office, the Lord Mayor resides at Mansion House and is supported by a staff. If the Lord Mayor has a young family, they may also reside in Mansion House, as was the case for Sir Christopher Leaver during his Mayoralty (1981-82), and more recently the Brewer family and dog (2005-06) and in 2012-2013 the youngest son of the Lady Mayoress.

The Lord Mayor holds many ancient rights and privileges that are unique to the office, and as with so much of the City's customs and ceremony, they are exercised with an assiduous eye to historical precedent. In times past the Lord Mayor was the only commoner to be given the password to the Tower of London (it changes every night), the only member of the Privy Council who does not automatically retire on demise of the Crown (i.e., death of a monarch), and the only person who may permit regiments to enter the City with their colours flying, drums beating and bayonets fixed. The Lord Mayor may also present children for admission to Christ's Hospital (the Bluecoat School).

The Lord Mayor ranks among the peers as an Earl[3], is entitled to wear a Robe of State similar to a peer's coronation robe and would be granted the burial rites of a peer if they died in the Sovereign's presence. The Lord Mayor has the status of a Cabinet Minister when on business overseas. On arriving for a banquet, dinner or other formal occasion at Mansion House or Guildhall, the Lord Mayor's arrival is signified by a trumpet fanfare, most often 'Fanfare for a dignified occasion' by Bliss.

The Lord Mayor has the right to a seat in the Peer's Gallery during the State Opening of Parliament, has a throne in St Paul's Cathedral on the left hand side of the choir, and is entitled to venison from the Royal Forest. The Lord Mayor may also request a private audience with the Sovereign at any time.

When the new Lord Mayor is elected, they first appear in public outside Guildhall accompanied by the Sheriffs and heralded by a fanfare of four state trumpeters of the Household Cavalry, which is another honour conferred by the Sovereign and unique to the Lord Mayor of London.

By custom the Lord Mayor is the first person to be informed of the death of the Monarch, and only the Lord Mayor has the authority to order the bells of St Paul's Cathedral to toll on the demise of the reigning Monarch. The Lord Mayor is also entitled

---

[3] The first life peer to be elected Lord Mayor of London was Baron Mais of Walbrook in 1972. The first hereditary peer to be elected Lord Mayor was Baron Mountevans of Chelsea in 2015. In past centuries some former Lord Mayors were elevated to the peerage following their term of office but it was by no means common or automatic.

to sit as a judge in the Central Criminal Court, as are the other Aldermen.

In modern times, the Lord Mayor is an ambassador for the City and the UK financial and professional services sectors in general and spends about one-third of their year overseas. The Lord Mayor also supports various charitable causes, usually reflecting their personal interests. In addition, the Lord Mayor acts as a spokesperson for the Livery, and as a practical matter, all Lord Mayors are members of one or more Livery Companies - unless they are a member of either the Ironmongers' Company or the Clothworkers' Company, neither of which permit their Freemen or Liverymen to be members of another Company.

Until the 1960s Lord Mayors were raised to the rank of Baronet on election; later they were invested as a Knight Grand Cross of The Most Excellent Order of the British Empire on election.

Past Lord Mayors are nowadays usually elevated to the rank of Knight Bachelor (in the case of men) or Dame of the Most Excellent Order of the British Empire (in the case of women) in the New Year Honours list after their year in office.

It is currently the custom that Lord Mayors are invested by the Sovereign as a Knight or Dame of Justice of the Order of St John on taking office[4]. This honour does not confer the title Sir or Dame but does confer post-nominal letters. The Lord Mayor will often receive decorations from foreign heads of state when on diplomatic business overseas during their year in office. Diplomatic gifts are also received and presented by the Lord Mayor, the latter paid for out of the Lord Mayor's pocket.

During the term of office the Lord Mayor cannot accept a directorship of a Company or appear in any prospectus of proposed directors for a Company, and in practice they are not able to engage in their profession during office.

---

[4] The headquarters of The Most Venerable Order of the Hospital of St John of Jerusalem is just outside the City at St John's Gate in Clerkenwell.

The privilege of dining out the Lord Mayor at the end of his or her year has long been held by the Goldsmiths' Company.

Lord Mayor Locum Tenens

Considering the Lord Mayor's hectic schedule of appointments within and outside the UK, they often cannot personally attend every function to which they are invited. This is particularly true for attending banquets at the Mansion House, a venue that has nearly 50,000 visitors each year. In such situations the Lord Mayor will often appoint a Locum Tenens from among the Aldermen who have passed the chair, i.e., those who have already served as Lord Mayor. The Lord Mayor Locum Tenens is addressed as such and carries the status, rights, privileges and authority of the Lord Mayor.

Representative Lord Mayor

A slightly different role to that described above, the Representative Lord Mayor is an Alderman who need not have passed the chair but who represents the Lord Mayor. Unlike the Lord Mayor Locum Tenens, the Representative Lord Mayor does not carry the status and authority of the Lord Mayor.

The Sheriffs

The office of Sheriff is the oldest in the City, dating back to at least the 7th century. The Livery elects two Sheriffs each year on Midsummer Day (24th June, the feast of St John the Baptist, or the next nearest weekday) for a one-year term of office from 28th September.

In April 2020 the Court of Common Council announced that the incumbent Sheriffs, Alderman & Professor Michael Mainelli and Common Councilman Christopher Hayward would continue in office for a second year because of the Covid-19 pandemic. The election of Sheriffs at Common Hall was also cancelled as the City has the power to elect and 'amove' Sheriffs as it wills.

One of the Sheriffs is usually an Alderman whilst the other is not. Since 1385 an Alderman seeking to become Lord Mayor must have previously been a Sheriff so as to be tried as to their *governance and bounty* before attaining the estate and dignity of the Mayoralty. Nothing stops a Sheriff who was elected whilst not an Alderman from being elected an Alderman at a later date, thereby satisfying that criterion for progression to the Mayoralty.

Occasionally when the pool of qualified Aldermen seeking to become Lord Mayor dwindles, the Court of Aldermen puts forward two Aldermanic Sheriffs in a year to replenish the pool. This arrangement is achieved with the agreement of the Livery through the Livery Committee.

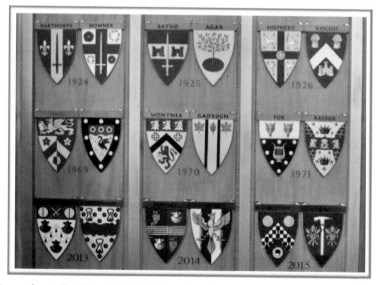

Arms of past Sheriffs on display in the Judges' dining room at the Old Bailey.

The Sheriffs support the Lord Mayor's year in office and attend the judges at the Old Bailey, for which purpose they have a residential complex in the Court.

If the candidates for Sheriff are not armigerous, they are expected to obtain a Grant of Arms prior to taking up office by petitioning the Earl Marshal through HM College of Arms, or The Court of Lord Lyon if the Sheriff resides in Scotland or has significant land and property there. The Sheriff's personal arms are then worked into a badge that also features the arms of the City of London and the Livery Companies of which they are a member, along with the arms of any other institutions with which they are connected (e.g., school, university, professional body). The badge is then suspended from a gold shrieval chain of three loops and it is the chain, not the badge, which is the symbol of office. The result is that every Sheriff's badge is a unique work of art, and nothing like the five-pointed tin star that features in cowboy films.

The Sheriffs also carry a sword, often a rapier or Court sword, as part of their uniform and in times past they were personally responsible for conducting judicial executions. This task they usually delegated to a hired executioner. Should the need arise, the Old Bailey has a number of suitable swords that the Sheriffs may borrow.

The Sheriffs are appointed by Royal Warrant, and the Monarch may stay their appointment after election. As a result all candidates for election to the office of Sheriffs must be subjects of the Crown. The Sheriffs Royal Warrant is presented during the Ceremony of the Quit Rents at the Royal Courts of Justice. A copy of the Warrant is displayed in the Old Bailey.

Each of the City's 25 wards is headed by an Alderman.

The Aldermen

The Aldermen were originally responsible for the good administration of the City and form the Court of Aldermen. The first recorded London Alderman, or Ealdorman, was Ethelred, son-in-law and appointee of King Alfred the Great.

The number of Aldermen has varied over time, and now there are 25, one for each of the electoral wards in the City. They are elected by the residents and business voters in each ward, and are required to meet the standard prescribed for Police and Crime Commissioners elsewhere in the UK, or be a Justice of the Peace. Nominally Aldermen are elected for life, although by modern convention they put themselves up for re-election every six years and retire on reaching 70 years of age. The Aldermen, when sitting in session with the Common Councilmen, form the City's governing body: The Court of Common Council.

The Aldermen have their own dedicated meeting room in the Guildhall complex. Looking rather like a lunar landing craft that is docked to the western side of Guildhall yard. The Aldermen's Court is used by the Lord Mayor and Aldermen for business which does not involve the whole Court of Common Council. Few people know that the Aldermen's Court is also used to host the meetings of The Bermuda Society in the UK.

The Aldermen regulate the formation of new Livery Companies, and have oversight of the granting of Royal Charters, in addition to other duties related to the Livery and Freedom. The title *Alderman* is of Anglo-Saxon origin and predates that of Lord Mayor. The Aldermen have two forms of ceremonial dress: fur-trimmed violet robes worn for Common Hall, and fur-trimmed scarlet robes worn for other ceremonial occasions such as the Lord Mayor's Show. Occasionally the Aldermen may be seen wearing bicorn hats.

The Aldermen's Court on the west side of Guildhall Yard would not look out of place in a 1970s science fiction film. Despite its modernist appearance the interior of the Court is decorated with the heraldic banners of those Aldermen who have served as Lord Mayor along with that of the current Lord Mayor.

Common Councilmen

The residents and businesses of the City of London elect the Common Councilmen. An election is held every four years, or as a vacancy arises owing to retirement, incapacity or death. The Common Councilmen perform much of the committee work, and together with the Aldermen, Aldermanic Sheriff and Lord Mayor form the Court of Common Council. The Common Councilmen wear robes of mazarine blue at the first council meeting after the installation of the Lord Mayor and on other special occasions.

Note: In March 2019 the Court of Common Council voted to change the usage of the title Common Councilman to Common Councillor in documents and communications. This was done to remove a perceived barrier to gender inclusion. The word Councilman is derived from the third person singular for one, as in one who counsels and does not refer to gender. The legal title of the office remains Common Councilman for all other purposes and is unchanged. There are no proposals to change the legal titles of Alderman, Freeman, Liveryman all of which import both genders, although some female Aldermen have styled themselves as Alderwomen.

The Recorder of London

The Recorder is the City's senior legal officer and a member of the Court of Aldermen, although not an elected Alderman. The Recorder is the Senior Judge at the Central Criminal Court, otherwise known as the Old Bailey. The Recorder also holds the title of High Steward of Southwark and summonses the City's Courts Leet Juries there to assemble. The City of London Corporation, with the approval of the Lord Chancellor, appoints the Recorder.

The Common Serjeant

This officer has a dual role as the second most senior permanent judge at the Old Bailey and as a High Officer of the City of London. It is the Common Serjeant who presides over the election of the Sheriffs and Common Hall. The Common Serjeant also deputises for the Recorder of London if the latter is unavailable to perform the civic duties of that office.

The City Remembrancer

The Remembrancer is the City's most senior Ceremonial Officer and represents the City in Parliament. The office was created in 1571 and was originally a link between the Monarch and the City, indeed the Remembrancer still has a vital role in communications between the City and the Royal Household. The Remembrancer is one of four law officers of the City and has the right to sit in the under-gallery of the House of Commons in the capacity of a 'Role A Parliamentary Agent'.

The Chief Commoner

Every year the Common Councilmen elect a Chief Commoner from among their number to act as a representative and champion of the rights and privileges of the Court of Common Council. The Chief Commoner also counsels other Common Councilmen on matters of the Court of Common Council's rights, responsibilities and efficient conduct. The role is a figurehead for the Common Council and is intended to recognise long and distinguished service to the City of London Corporation. As with all the elected members of the Court of Common Council, the position is unsalaried and receives no personal expenses although an entertaining allowance is available as the Chief Commoner hosts varied guests at Guildhall during the year.

The Chief Commoner is granted a grace and favour apartment in Guildhall should he or she need it, and has several unusual duties including that of reviewing the plans for the demise of the Monarch.

As so often with the City's nomenclature and traditions, the title can cause confusion. On an official visit to China with the Lord Mayor, the Chief Commoner was erroneously introduced as 'Chief Peasant'.

The Town Clerk

The City of London Corporation has its own Chief Executive Officer in the Town Clerk. The most senior salaried employee of the Corporation, the Town Clerk is responsible for the efficient running of the functions of the City of London Corporation. It is curious that the office is so named considering that London has always been a City, although in mediaeval times the office was titled Common Clerk.

The Chamberlain

The Chamberlain is the Chief Finance Officer of the City of London Corporation. This officer has a special role in supporting the Court of Aldermen to advise on the formation of new City of London Livery Companies and in interpreting and amending their charters and ordinances. The Chamberlain's Court (a Court of Law located at Guildhall) is responsible for conducting the ceremony to admit persons into the Freedom of the City of London.

The Comptroller and City Solicitor

The origins of this office can be traced as far back as 1311. The Comptroller and City Solicitor is the senior legal officer of the City of London Corporation and heads a department that has responsibility for property transactions, employment law, planning issues, Freedom of Information requests and general litigation. As with so many other City officers, the Comptroller and City Solicitor also has several ceremonial duties, including participation in the ceremony of the Quit Rents.

The City Surveyor

This officer runs an immensely diverse portfolio of City lands and property. The portfolio of over 620 properties extends far beyond the Square Mile and even beyond the metropolis into the Home Counties. The City Surveyor oversees the use of the City's extensive property assets for investment, development, commerce, leisure and housing.

The Secondary of London and Under-Sheriff

This officer has responsibility for the day-to-day running of the Central Criminal Court (the Old Bailey) including security and maintenance. One of the duties of the Under-Sheriff is to assist the Sheriff in hosting the judges during lunch. The Under-Sheriff also serves as the High Bailiff of the three City manors in Southwark and swears in their officers at the Courts Leet.

The Ale Conners

This ancient office, elected by the Livery, is responsible for testing the wholesomeness, measure and pricing of ale and beer served in the Square Mile; no doubt a much sought-after office. In medieval times when fermentation was a vital way to prevent the spread of waterborne diseases, the Ale Conner had a crucial role in public health. As many as four Ale Conners are elected at Common Hall each year if there are vacancies.

In times past the Ale Conners would test beer at Inns in the City, and as late as 1949 the Lord Mayor, accompanied by the Master of the Brewers' Company, and two Ale Conners conducted an Ale Conning (testing) ceremony at the Tiger Tavern by the Tower of London. Following a fanfare by State Trumpeters of the Household Cavalry, the Ale Conners sampled the beer and declared it of good quality. The Lord Mayor hoisted a garland outside the Inn as a sign that the beer within had been found fit for consumption.

Another way the Ale Conners test the quality of Ale is by wearing leather trousers and sitting on a wooden stool soaked with the ale; if the leather trousers stick, the ale is deemed not to be of good quality as it contains too much sugar. This curious practice continues to be conducted from time to time.

An Upper Ale Conner and Under Ale Conner, and a Carniter (tester of meat) are appointed in the Guildable Manor of Southwark.

The Bridge Masters

Until 1855 this office was responsible for the receipt of rents from the Bridge House Estate, in addition to maintenance and upkeep of the City's bridges. Nowadays the role is honorary and ceremonial. Two Bridge Masters are elected each year, usually in an uncontested election. The Bridge House Estate still exists and has a special mark to denote its property; whilst it remains responsible for five bridges across the Thames, surplus funds (20 million pounds in 2018) are used for charitable purposes through the City Bridge Foundation.

The Ward Beadles

Each of the 25 wards of the City of London elects at least one Ward Beadle, although the three largest wards elect more than one each. The Beadles are elected on nomination of the Aldermen at a Wardmote (meeting of the ward voters); their duties include opening and closing the Wardmotes and accompanying their Aldermen at eight annual ceremonial occasions of the City. The Ward Beadles each carry a staff of office that differs in design from one ward to the next, as do their ceremonial robes.

The Keeper of Walbrook Hall

Few Liverymen will have heard of this officer or know of the whereabouts of the mysterious Walbrook Hall. It is simply the street level entrance to Mansion House on Walbrook. The Keeper assists in running Mansion House and welcomes everyone from heads of state to the general public. The Keeper also conducts weekly tours of Mansion House that last about an hour.

The Pageantmaster

This officer is responsible for the planning and smooth delivery of the annual Lord Mayor's Show. At the time of writing, the current Pageantmaster, Dominic Reid OBE, holds the record for the number of Lord Mayor's Shows organised during his term of office, topping the previous record that his father held! The office of the Pageantmaster has become more important and visible with the advent of television. The City renamed a street, Pageantmaster Court, after this officer in 1993.

Esquires of the Lord Mayor's Household

The Court of Aldermen appoints various other City Officers. Three particular officers of note are the Esquires of the Lord Mayor's Household, who help to arrange the Lord Mayor's complex and extensive programme and have additional major ceremonial roles. In the past, they were often been retired military officers.

The Esquires are as follows:

The Swordbearer of London

This officer carries the Sword of State in procession before the Lord Mayor as a symbol of authority and keeps the keys to the City of London Seal in a special pocket on the underside of their Muscovy hat, known as the 'Cap of Maintenance'.

The Common Cryer and Serjeant-at-Arms

This office is so old that the precise date of creation is unknown, but certainly before 1338. This officer carries the Great Mace before the Lord Mayor in procession. In addition to the Great Mace of Government, the Lord Mayor has their own mace or Crystal Sceptre, which was a gift from Henry V for the City's financial and material support to his campaign in France.

The City Marshal

This quasi-military officer was responsible for keeping the peace in the City before the creation of the City of London Police. In addition to heading up the Lord Mayor's procession, the City Marshal escorts those military units allowed the privilege of marching in the City with colours flying, drums beating and bayonets fixed (see the chapter, "The City and the Armed Forces").

The City Marshal in the Lord Mayor's Show

In times past there were two other Esquires of Mansion House: The Common Hunt and The Water Bailiff, the former keeping the City's pack of hounds and the latter responsible for water conservancy on the Thames and Medway rivers including the issuing of fishing licences and seizing of unlawful nets.

As the time of writing there are moves afoot in the Mansion House to appoint an Honorary Water Bailiff, who will be the 4th Esquire of the Mansion House.

While not one of the Esquires of the Mansion House, the Lord Mayor has a Private Secretary who is appointed by the Court of Aldermen.

City Ceremonial and Customs

There is no place in England in which old customs have been more carefully preserved than the square mile known as the City of London, and within its boundaries there are probably enshrined more of these ancient habits and survivals than any other place in the world.

George C. Williamson, *Curious Survivals 1922*

The Lord Mayor's Coach is pulled by six horses. By ancient custom a bunch of carrots is carried in the coach during the Lord Mayor's Show for the horses to eat during the break when the Lord Mayor is at the Royal Courts of Justice. Photograph courtesy of Christopher Histed.

The Cycle of Ceremonies

The Lord Mayor's Show is the most spectacular of the City's ceremonies and is the culmination of a series of civic ceremonies in the City's year. Their rhythm can be summarised as follows:

Election of Sheriffs

The sequence starts with the election of the two Sheriffs 'for the year ensuing' at Common Hall on Midsummer Day (24th June, or if a weekend, the Monday following) after which they become 'Sheriff Elect'.

Sheriffs receive their Royal Warrant

The Sheriffs attend the Royal Courts of Justice to swear an oath of allegiance to the Monarch and receive their Royal Warrant. This is displayed in the Old Bailey during their year in office. This ceremony is conducted with the Ceremony of the Quit Rents and is usually held on or near to St Michael's Day (October 11).

Sheriffs Take Office

The day before the Mayoral election, the Sheriffs take office at a public ceremony with invited guests at Guildhall. They read a declaration in unison and sign a register. Following this the Sheriffs host a breakfast (like a wedding breakfast) on Michaelmas Eve (unless a weekend) and give a speech to an extensive audience of guests, including all living former Sheriffs.

Election of Lord Mayor

Election of the Lord Mayor 'for the year ensuing' takes place at Common Hall on Michaelmas Day (29th September or if a weekend, the nearest weekday). The Alderman so elected becomes 'Lord Mayor Elect'. The Lord Mayor Elect's wife then becomes the Lady Mayoress Designate, offering a brief period of six weeks during which the Lord Mayor Elect might choose an alternative! Presumably the same applies to the consort of a female Lord Mayor Elect.

Presentation of the Lord Mayor to the Lord Chancellor

Once elected the Lord Mayor must receive the approbation of the Monarch. This is delivered by the Lord Chancellor during a ceremony held in the House of Lords. The ceremony includes a loving cup and the sharing of shortbread. The Lord Chancellor makes a speech welcoming the Lord Mayor.

Lord Mayor Takes Office

The new Lord Mayor takes office at the 'Silent Ceremony' on the Friday preceding the second Saturday in November.

Lord Mayor's Show

The day after taking office (i.e., second Saturday in November) the Lord Mayor processes through the City to swear allegiance to the Sovereign in front of Her Majesty's Justices.

The Mayoral Team is now complete until the cycle starts again next Midsummer Day.

The Lord Mayor's Show

The Lord Mayor travels in procession to the Royal Courts of Justice to swear an oath to the Sovereign. The Lord Mayor's Show is the world's largest unrehearsed pageant, typically involving over 6,000 participants and weaving its way through the City in a 3.5-mile-long procession of marching bands and civic, charitable, corporate, school and Livery Company floats. The Lord Mayor's Show also features many military units, and more service personnel than Trooping the Colour.

Curiously, when the Lord Mayor presents himself or herself to the judges at the Royal Courts of Justice, they don black caps, as was the custom when passing a death sentence! Perhaps this is why the Dean of St Paul's Cathedral blesses the Lord Mayor during a brief pause in the procession. The term *float* derives from the Lord Mayor's Show formerly being held on the River Thames, giving rise to the designation of vehicles in the procession as 'floats'.

Watermen and their Bargemaster still participate in the Lord Mayor's Show and process ahead of the Lord Mayor's state coach

From 2011-2017 the Lord Mayor's Flotilla returned as an annual element of the Show proceeding from Westminster Bridge to HMS President by St Katharine Docks on the early morning of the show. The Lord Mayor travelled aboard HM The King's Royal Barge Gloriana which was rowed by members of the Watermen and Lightermen's Company and accompanied on the river by cutters of the various Livery Companies usually carrying their respective Masters. The flotilla terminated at the Royal Navy Reserve (RNR) shore station, HMS President, where the Lord Mayor, as Admiral of the Port of London, was received by the commander of HMS President and inspects a guard of honour. This event has since been replaced by the Lord Mayor's River Progress which takes place in September.

While at HMS President, the Master of the Coopers' Company joins the Lord Mayor, Sheriffs and other Livery Company Masters for the Rum Ceremony. This ceremony involves the Master Cooper presenting a barrel of rum to the officers and crew in recognition of the Coopers' Company's affiliation with the RNR shore station since the early 1970s. The toast on this occasion is 'up spirits' and gathered dignitaries and ship's company wish the Lord Mayor good luck for their year in office.

The Lord Mayor doesn't always ride in a golden coach. The Lord Mayor's official car is a Rolls-Royce Phantom VI sporting the number plate LM O.

The Lord Mayor's Banquet

This event is held at Guildhall on the Monday after the Lord Mayor's Show and is given in honour of the Late Lord Mayor, i.e., the immediate past Lord Mayor. The Prime Minister, The Archbishop of Canterbury and the Lord Chancellor attend the banquet and each of them delivers a speech to the City and gathered dignitaries.

A series of annual banquets is held at Mansion House including one for the bankers and merchants of the City of London at which the Chancellor of the Exchequer gives a keynote speech; one for the Livery Company Masters, Prime Wardens and Upper Bailiff; one for the judges; one for the Mayors and Chief Executives of the London governing bodies; another for the diplomatic corps; and one every other year for the Bishops.

State Banquets for Foreign Heads of State

Guildhall is also the scene for banquets in honour of foreign Heads of State visiting London. By custom any visiting Heads of State to the United Kingdom are first hosted by the Sovereign at Buckingham Palace or Windsor Castle and then by the Lord Mayor of London at Guildhall.

The Election of the Lord Mayor

As mentioned, the Lord Mayor is elected on Michaelmas Day (29th September or the nearest weekday). The gathering at which the Livery approve two candidates and the Aldermen make the final selection is known as 'Common Hall'. The Liverymen of the City Livery Companies approve the candidates for Lord Mayor by acclamation (although exceptionally a ballot may be called) after which the Aldermen withdraw to make their selection between the approved candidates. The Aldermen each receive a ballot paper on which they write the name of their preferred candidate.

During the ballot the City's sword is place in a bed of roses in the Aldermen's Court.

Presentation of the Lord Mayor to the Lord Chancellor

This is a private ceremony held in October at the House of Lords. The Lord Mayor Elect is presented to the Lord Chancellor, who gives Her Majesty's approbation to the City's choice of Chief Magistrate. Following a speech by the Lord Chancellor a Loving Cup is shared and by tradition a piece of shortbread. The only other persons present are usually the two Sheriffs and the Lord Mayor Elect's husband, wife or consort.
In theory this event provides the opportunity for the Monarch to stay the installation of the Lord Mayor and require the City to choose another candidate. In times past the scabbard to the City's sword would be retained by the Lord Chancellor thereby indicating that the Monarch could sheath the sword at any time, thereby removing the Lord Mayor's authority.

The Silent Ceremony

This ceremony takes place at Guildhall on the Friday before the second Saturday in November when the retiring Lord Mayor hands over to the Lord Mayor Elect. The Lord Mayor's ceremonial regalia are presented to the incoming Lord Mayor. The ceremony is conducted in silence with the exception of the declaration made by the new Lord Mayor. After the ceremony the City Swordbearer passes one of the three keys to the City Seal to the Late Lord Mayor, who passes it to the newly elected Lord Mayor, who then returns it to the City Swordbearer, who agrees to *keep it under their hat*.

Presentation of Gifts to the Lord Mayor

Many of the City Livery Companies present gifts to the Lord
Mayor and Lady Mayoress or consort. A few examples include: a
boar's head *caput apri defero* from the Butchers, gloves from the
Glovers, a pen from the Scriveners, spectacles from the Spectacle
Makers, a barrel of rum from the Coopers, fruit from the
Fruiterers, the Lord Mayor's tricorn hat from the Feltmakers,
and so on. The Lord Mayor will also receive gifts from foreign
heads of state when they visit Mansion House or when the Lord
Mayor travels overseas, and the Lord Mayor (who is unsalaried)
is expected to give appropriate gifts in return.

The Election of the Sheriffs

The Liverymen of the City Livery Companies elect two Sheriffs
annually on Midsummer Day at Guildhall. One Sheriff is usually
elected from among the Aldermen of the City of London, and
thereby becomes eligible to stand for election as Lord Mayor in
the future. The other Sheriff is normally elected from among the
Livery and is sometimes known as the Non-Aldermanic (or in the
past Lay) Sheriff. At times two Aldermen have been elected as
Sheriffs in the same year in order to ensure a steady supply of
candidates for Lord Mayor.

The Sheriffs' Breakfast

The Sheriffs' Breakfast is held in late September and
immediately preceded by a short ceremony conducted in
Guildhall. During the ceremony the outgoing Sheriffs place the
chains of office on the incoming Sheriffs in the presence of the
Lord Mayor. Oaths to the King and the City of London are read

by the newly installed Sheriffs after which the civic party processes to Guildhall Yard for photos.

Newly installed Sheriffs with the Lord Mayor, Sword Bearer, Common Cryer & Serjeant at Arms, the City Marshal and the Lord Mayor's Chaplain

This ceremony is followed by the Sheriffs' Breakfast - a serious repast with speeches from both Sheriffs and a guest of honour. Guests are advised not to expect to rise before 3.30pm.

An Aldermanic Sheriff who subsequently goes on to become Lord Mayor may obtain an amended shrieval badge to include a crossed sword and mace behind the coat of arms in the centre of the badge.

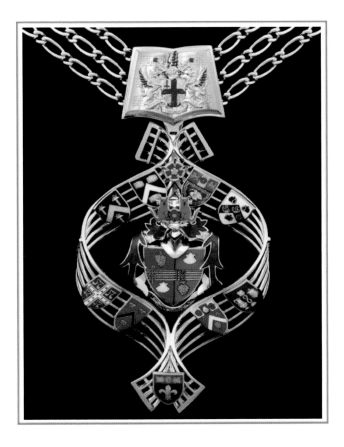

Shrieval badge of Alderman Sir Andrew Parmley, featuring his personal arms in the centre, surrounded by those of organisations with which he is connected. Photograph courtesy of Alderman Sir Andrew Parmley.

Rendering of the Quit Rents to the Crown

This is the second oldest ceremony in the realm, with only the Coronation being more ancient. It takes place on a date between 11th October and 11th November. During this ceremony the City pays several ancient rents to the Crown in respect of various lands it rents. The ceremony takes place at the Royal Courts of Justice and the Crown is represented by an officer of state known as the King's Remembrancer. One of the rents is paid with six horseshoes and 61 nails, the other with two billhooks-knives, one sharp, the other blunt.

This is also the occasion at which the incoming Sheriffs are presented to the King's Remembrancer by the Under Sheriff and Common Serjeant and receive their Royal Warrants. Since the ceremony is held as a Court meeting it is open for members of the public to observe the ceremony.

Swan Upping

This ceremony takes place on the River Thames over five days each summer, usually in mid-July. The Crown shares the right to mark swans with the Vintners' Company and the Dyers' Company and the Ilchester family who maintain the world's only breeding colony at Abbotsbury in Dorset. Originally the swans were destined for the banqueting table and the two ancient Companies share the right to serve swan with certain Oxford and Cambridge colleges of royal foundation. The swan upping ceremony dates from the 12th century. In the past the Vintners' Company marked the bills (not beaks) of their swans with two nicks. Those of the Dyers' Company were marked with one nick; in modern times the swans are marked with one or two rings; those that remain unmarked are the property of the Crown. Should you ever see a pub called *The Swan with Two Necks* (of which there are several in England) you might wish to pop in and tell the landlord that it should be 'Two Nicks'.

To celebrate Queen Elizabeth II's Diamond Jubilee in 2012 an educational brochure 'Royal Swan Upping' was produced. The brochure is available online.

The Swan Warden's Banner of the Vintners' Company on display in Vintners' Hall.

The Trial of the Pyx

This ceremony dates from 1249 and is held at Goldsmiths' Hall. It is one of the extant regulatory responsibilities still conducted by a City Livery Company and is the oldest independent quality control process in the world.

The Trial process starts when the King's Remembrancer swears in a jury of 26 Goldsmiths who count, weigh and measure a sample of 88,000 coins of the realm produced by the Royal Mint. From these sample coins the jury select a random sample to be tested for weight, dimensions, metallic composition and fineness. The term 'Pyx' refers to the box in which these coins are kept, and derives from the Pyx chapel at Westminster Abbey where religious vestments were stored. The trial usually starts on the second Thursday in February and the verdict is announced in May.

It is not widely known that the Trial of the Pyx also tests the coinage of New Zealand, which is also minted in the UK.

Founder's Day - Sir John Cass School

Otherwise known as Red Feather Day, this event celebrates Sir John Cass, founder of the eponymous City school. On or around 20th February (Sir John Cass's birthday) pupils from the school, along with City dignitaries, attend a church service at St Botolph without Aldgate, each wearing a symbolic red feather. The feather represents a blood-stained quill pen because Sir John Cass died of a brain haemorrhage whilst writing his will.

Sir John was an Alderman, Sheriff and MP for the City. He founded a school for 50 boys and 40 girls in 1710. Because he died writing his will, it was contested, and it took another 30 years to resolve the matter. His will left money and property to the school, which continues to benefit from his endowment.

Presentation of the Pearl Sword

When the Sovereign enters the City on ceremonial occasions, the Lord Mayor greets the Sovereign at the City boundary, eg. at the old site of Temple Bar. The Lord Mayor presents the Pearl Sword of the City to the Sovereign in token of the City's loyalty; the Sovereign acknowledges the Lord Mayor's authority by touching the sword. A variant of this ceremony takes place when a new Sovereign is proclaimed by one of the Officers of Arms who is met at Temple Bar by the City Marshal. The real Temple Bar, the last of the City's gateways, is now located near St Paul's Cathedral at the southern entrance of Paternoster Square after languishing in the grounds of Theobalds Park from 1880 until 1984.

On other occasions when the Sovereign attends an event in the City, the Lord Mayor will meet and greet the Sovereign and introduce dignitaries as a Lord Lieutenant would do in one of the counties.

Remembrance Day Service

The Masters of the several Livery Companies join the annual Garden of Remembrance Service located on the North-East side of St Paul's Cathedral in early November. Following a short service the Masters plant small crosses in the lawn of the garden.

A painting by Talbot Rice now hanging in Ironmongers' Hall showing the presentation of the Pearl Sword of the City of London to Queen Elizabeth II at Temple Bar. This scene was enacted by former Lord Mayor Sir Michael Oliver during the Queen's Golden Jubilee procession.

Cart Marking

The Worshipful Company of Carmen exercise the right to licence and mark *carrs* and carts that may stand and ply for hire in the City's streets. This ceremony, which involves many historic vehicles, takes place annually at Guildhall Yard during the summer and is open to the public to attend.

During this ceremony the Master Carman, aided by the Keeper of Guildhall and various City dignitaries, uses a branding iron to mark a wooden plate affixed to a selection of circa 50 vehicles, some horse-drawn, some steam-powered, and others more

modern conveyances. The vehicle owner must be a Freeman of
the City of London and a member of the Carmen's Company.
Vehicles are branded with a letter which indicates the year in
which they were marked. The Glovers' Company, always keen to
get its fingers into another ceremony, provides suitable gloves for
the Keeper of Guildhall and the Master Carman to wear whilst
holding the branding iron. In the custom of the Livery
Companies, the ceremony is followed by a drinks reception and
lunch at Guildhall.

A vehicle marking plate scorched with the shield of the arms of the City of
London and yearly licence letters. The letter 'Y' indicates a mark applied in 2016.

Driving on the Left

Traffic across the old London Bridge became so congested in the
early 18th century that a Lord Mayor ordered all traffic entering
London from the south to keep to the left-hand side of the
bridge, and all traffic headed from the north to do likewise. This
may be why we still drive on the left in the UK, Ireland and many
Commonwealth countries to this day.

Opening of Bartholomew Fair

The Hand and Shears pub on the corner of Cloth Fair and Middle Street was for many centuries the scene of the opening of the annual Bartholomew Fair by the Lord Mayor on the eve of the feast of St Bartholomew (August 24th). This ancient charter market dating from 1133 was declared open when the Lord Mayor used a pair of shears to cut a length of cloth that was stretched across Cloth Fair. Bartholomew Fair died out in the 1850s but the custom of opening events by cutting a ribbon with scissors continues.

The Inter-Livery Pancake Races

Hosted by the Worshipful Company of Poulters, this annual event takes place on Shrove Tuesday at Guildhall Yard with the support of The Cook & The Butler City caterers. The Masters and Clerks of many of the City Livery Companies together with representatives of other City institutions, such as the Old Bailey, join in friendly competition in various races for Masters, Liverymen and Fancy Dress.

The winning Company in each race receives a copper frying pan which is immediately engraved with the name of the winning Company for that year.

The Musicians' Company recently commissioned a song to be sung during the races.

A luncheon for the competitors and supporters is held in the Guildhall crypt after the races. Tickets are available from The Cook & The Butler.

The Prime Warden of the Basketmakers' Company participating in the Inter-Livery Pancake Race on Shrove Tuesday 2014.

John Stow Memorial Service and Ceremony of Changing the Quill

The Worshipful Company of Merchant Taylors and the London & Middlesex Archaeological Society sponsor this event. It celebrates the life of John Stow, a former member of The Merchant Taylors' Company who wrote the Survey of London in 1598. The service (formerly held annually, in the presence of the Lord Mayor and the Ward of Aldgate dignitaries) is now held every three years in the presence of the Aldermen of the Ward of Cornhill, on or around 5th April, at St Andrew Undershaft and features an address in honour of Stow, and the placing of a new quill pen in the hand of Stow's effigy, preceded by a church service.

Admiral of the Port's Challenge

The Lord Mayor is, among many other offices, the Admiral of the Port of London, albeit that no uniform goes with the role. Nevertheless, the Lord Mayor is still piped aboard Her Majesty's ship in the manner befitting an Admiral.

The Admiral of the Port's Challenge exists to promote and encourage the sport of rowing and sculling using cutters (a long rowing boat) that meet the specifications laid down by the Company of Watermen and Lightermen. The race is held over 1.33 miles between the Palace of Westminster and the Westminster Boating Base.

Those Livery Companies that are members of the Thames Traditional Rowing Association participate in this annual event. It is a requirement that the cutters carry two passengers under a raised canopy and fly the heraldic banner of the Livery Company.

Each cutter is 34 feet long and 4 feet 6 inches wide, and may be crewed by up to six oarsmen along with a cox and several passengers.

Port of London Challenge

This event was first held in 1996 and is now an annual fixture in which the cutters of the Thames Traditional Rowing Association participate. The course runs from HQS Wellington (the former Livery Hall of the Master Mariners' Company) to Chelsea Harbour, 4.4 miles away.

Doggett's Coat and Badge Wager

This is an annual competitive rowing race on the River Thames held over 4 miles and 7 furlongs. First held in 1715, the race is believed to be the oldest continuously contested sporting event in the world (2015 marked its 300th anniversary). The race is named after its founder and benefactor, the Irish actor Thomas Doggett. He was supposedly a Liveryman of the Worshipful Company of Fishmongers, although no records of his membership survive.

The race is open to Freemen of the Company of Watermen and Lightermen in their first, second or third year of Freedom. The race takes the form of a competitive single sculling competition from London Bridge to Chelsea Bridge (originally from the Swan Inn at London Bridge to the Swan Inn at Chelsea Bridge, but neither of these establishments exists today). The prize for winning the race is a red coat and a large silver badge bearing the symbol of the House of Hanover and the word 'Liberty'.

Doggett originally managed the race until his death in 1721. Since then the Worshipful Company of Fishmongers has overseen the competition. Winners of the race usually go on to join the ranks of the King's Watermen and row the skiffs used by the Vintners' and Dyers' Companies during the annual Swan Upping on the Thames.

Freemen of the City of London exercising their right to take livestock across London Bridge without incurring tolls. The shepherds in this photograph are led by the Master Woolman.

Sheep Drive across London Bridge

The right to exemption from tolls when taking goods and livestock across London Bridge was an important privilege of Freemen in times past. Since wool was an important source of the nation's wealth, the practice of driving sheep across London Bridge became synonymous with this right. In recent years, to raise funds for charity.

Several Livery Companies and charities (World Traders, Tax Advisers, Woolmen and the City Branch of the Red Cross) have organised sheep drives across London Bridge at a weekend during which Freemen may exercise their ancient right and receive a certificate as evidence of their shepherding skills. The sheep drive is now an annual event organised by the Woolmen's Company and has its own website for advance booking. The event is usually opened by a celebrity Freeman. In past years such notable persons as Mary Berry CBE, Dame Barbara Windsor and Nigel Mansell CBE have opened the event.

The Loving Cup Ceremony forms part of the ceremonial at Livery Company Banquets. Photograph courtesy of Christopher Histed.

Livery Company Ceremonial

The Livery Companies maintain their own rich tapestry of customs and ceremonial, some unique to specific Companies, such as the Cocks and Caps ceremony of the Skinners in which the Master is elected by trying the Master's cap on several members, and 'if the cap fits' he or she wears it (as if by magic, the cap fits only the candidate to be Master). There are similar caps for each of the Wardens. After the cap is found to fit, toasts are drunk to the new Master from cockerel-shaped goblets.

The Basketmakers use a wicker Griffin's head as their Beadle's staff of office. The Griffin is one of the heraldic supporters of the Company's coat of arms. The Griffin's head precedes the Prime Warden and other officers of the Company when in procession. The Company also has a heraldic banner which follows the procession. Possibly the rarest processional artefact belongs to the Horners' Company, which proudly displays a Narwhal's tusk at the head of its procession.

The Skinners and Merchant Taylors share a ceremony when they alternate position in the order of precedence by their Masters exchanging gavels. The Barbers have a series of garlands (ornately decorated coronets) that are presented to the Master and Wardens on election but never worn. The Tobacco Pipe Makers and Tobacco Blenders has a particularly apt ceremony known as the Smoking Cap Ceremony, although they no longer issue pipes and cigars. The Bowyers offer a toast to a former member that is conducted in silence.

The Water Conservators even conduct a Ceremony of Passing Water, although they do not say whether this happens before or after dinner!

Many Companies have their own song, with notable examples being those of the Grocers' Company, the Vintners' Company and the Master's song of the Broderers' Company sung as a solo!

Most Companies use a standard form of sung Grace after dinner, taken from 'Laudi Spirituali' of 1545, which is sung by all present.

Several other ceremonies are common to most Companies but interpreted in slightly different ways, such as the Loving Cup Ceremony (during which the Distillers' Company hold daggers), at Livery Company dinners and banquets; the Livery Clothing Ceremony at which Freemen are elevated to Liverymen; and the Rose Bowl Ceremony, where two separate activities were merged into one during the Victorian era: washing of hands in rose water and stimulating the Alderman's nerve with a moistened towel to help digestion (with scientific support).

Most formal events start with a receiving line where the Master and Wardens receive members and their guests after the Beadle has formally announced them.

For guidance on the formalities of City banquets, the Actuaries' Company provides a handy guide to etiquette at Livery Company dinners on their website, and other Livery Companies have their own versions. A comprehensive guide to formal and semi-formal dress appropriate for City and Livery Company banquets is in Appendix B of this guide, along with the etiquette for passing the port in Appendix D.

The Boar's Head Ceremony

Every year in early December the Worshipful Company of Butchers presents a Boar's Head to the Lord Mayor at Mansion House, after processing through the streets of London with the Boar's Head on a tray held at shoulder height, usually with a police escort and marching band. The Boar's Head nowadays is a papier-maché mock-up with the real cooked boar's head having been taken to Mansion House earlier in the day. The Cutlers' Company holds a traditional Boar's Head Feast in December.

Joint Archery Shoot at the Tower of London

This annual event was started in the mid-1970s and is held at different times each year. It brings together two Companies that split in the 14th century because of arguments over demarcation of responsibilities. The Bowyers' Company and the Fletchers' Company meet for a day of light-hearted competitive archery in the moat of HM Tower of London, after which they enjoy a convivial meal, usually in the mess of the Royal Fusiliers, where they put their past enmity to rest - until the next year.

Beating of the Bounds and The Tower Hill Battle

A custom associated with All Hallows by the Tower is the annual Beating of the Bounds. Many City churches continue the custom of marking the parish boundaries by processing with hazel branches, canes, or some other artefact suitable for 'beating' the boundary of the parish.

All Hallows continues this tradition yearly, while every three years they meet with the Governor and Yeoman Warders outside the Tower to engage in a 'battle', now a friendly exchange, that recalls an incident in 1698 when a great tumult and riot took place between the parishioners and the Tower authorities. The beating of the bounds takes place on Ascension Day.

Vintners 'Installation Service

The Vintners' Company has a curious custom that takes place before the installation service of their Master Elect at the Church of St James Garlickhythe. The Master, Wardens and other members of the Company process from Vintners' Hall preceded by one or more Wine Porters who sweep the street with a birch broom. The Master, Wardens and other officers of the Company hold posies of sweet-smelling flowers. This custom derives from the time when London's streets were filthy and the air foul-smelling.

The Knollys Rose Ceremony

The church of All Hallows by the Tower is the start point for this annual ceremony in which a single red rose is picked from the garden on Seething Lane and placed on a velvet altar cushion. The rose is then carried in procession by the Verger of All Hallows along with members of the Company of Watermen and Lightermen to Mansion House and presented to the Lord Mayor. The rose is presented in payment of a fine, or more accurately a Quit Rent, which was levied on Sir Robert Knollys (pronounced Knowles) after his wife Lady Constance Knollys built a footbridge between two properties on Seething Lane without permission in 1381. The ceremony usually takes place on the second Monday in June but may vary from year to year depending on the Lord Mayor's diary.

Oiling of the Gates at Temple Bar

Since the Chartered Architects took out a lease on Temple Bar in Paternoster Square they have instituted a new ceremony conducted in May whereby the Master ensures the smooth opening of the gates by oiling the hinges.

Note: The dates and locations of selected City ceremonies are given in Appendix E.

Places to Visit in the City

By seeing London I have seen as much of life as the world can show.

Dr Samuel Johnson

The City is home to many institutions of national and global importance, too numerous to mention in full.

Many other landmarks in the City, both public and private, are amply served by a wealth of popular tourist guidebooks to the City. The City Information Centre, mentioned at the end of this chapter, is the best source of information on places of interest, events, guided tours, open days and self-guided walking trails around the City.

What follows is a selection of notable places to visit that are associated with the history and governance of the City.

Mansion House

Mansion House serves as both a centre for civic hospitality and home to the Lord Mayor. Its frontage forms the shortest street in the City – Mansion House Street.

Mansion House is home to the Lord Mayor of London and is the setting for many state banquets and civic dinners in its splendid Egyptian Hall. Mansion House was built between 1739 - 1752 and has an extensive collection of silver and gold plate, probably the best in the world, as well as the Harold Samuel Collection of Dutch and Flemish 17th century paintings, which that philanthropist bequeathed to beautify the building. It also features several prison cells from the days when Mansion House was the home of the City of London Magistrates' Court, until the mid-1980s. The housekeeper of Mansion House is known as the Keeper of Walbrook Hall.

Qualified City of London guides run a weekly tour of Mansion House on Tuesdays, except in August. Tours are limited to 40 people and operate on a first-come, first-served basis. The tour lasts for one hour and it is always best to check in advance that the tour is going ahead as other events at Mansion House may cause changes to the tour schedule. Cost £9.50 (2019 rates).

A Livery Company White Tie banquet in the Egyptian Hall of Mansion House. Photograph courtesy of The Worshipful Company of Information Technologists.

Guildhall is the seat of the City's government, the Court of Common Council.

Guildhall

Qualified City of London guides conduct a one-hour tour of Guildhall, exploring many parts of this early medieval building that are not generally open to the public. The tour covers the history of Guildhall, the governance of the City of London and many of the historical figures connected with the City, including Dick Whittington. This is where the original hustings or hus þing (*house thing*) took place, meaning a meeting of the household. The names of all the Lord Mayors of London may be seen in the stained-glass windows all around the Great Hall. Cost £10 (2019 rates).

Note: The tours take place every day that the Court of Common Council meets, and visitors are welcome to stay for the Court meeting in the public gallery of Guildhall.

The Court of Common Council

The Court of Common Council is the elected governance body of the City of London. It comprises 100 Common Councilmen and 25 Aldermen (one for each ward of the City). The businesses and residents in the City elect the Common Councilmen and

Aldermen. By tradition all the Common Councilmen and Aldermen are independent; political parties do not operate in the City and are not recognised by the Corporation, party agents and whips are not permitted, party names do not appear on ballot papers, seats on committees are not allocated on a party basis.

The Court meets nine times a year and members of the public are welcome to attend. The last meeting of the year is significant since the new Lord Mayor of the City of London chairs the meeting for the first time and all the Councilmen and Aldermen dress up in their ceremonial robes, scarlet for the Aldermen and mazarine blue for the Common Councilmen. Free entry.

Guildhall Art Gallery

Guildhall Art Gallery houses the City of London's extensive art collection, only a fraction of which is on display at any time. The Gallery boasts both classical and modern paintings, busts, statues and other art works, many of which relate to the history of the City. The basement of Guildhall Art Gallery also houses the ruins of the Roman Amphitheatre that lie underneath the Guildhall courtyard. Guided tours of the collection run on Tuesdays, Fridays and Saturdays at 12:15, 14:15, 15:15 and 16:15. Free entry and tour.

The Museum of London (Partly Closed)

The Museum of London charts the history of London from Roman to modern times. It is widely recognised as one of the best museums in the UK. The Lord Mayor's Coach is kept on display in the public galleries (except in the week before the Lord Mayor's Show) along with various items of City and Livery Company regalia. There is also a section on the ancient craft Guilds and their role in the development of the City in medieval times. The museum also has an extensive online archive of photographs of exhibits including Livery Company badges of office. Free entry.

Note: At the time of publishing the Museum of London has announced an intention to relocate its main premises to West Smithfield, reopening in 2026. Once the move is complete the museum will be renamed The London Museum, meanwhile the Museum of London Docklands site remains open.

The City Information Centre

Located in St Paul's churchyard on the south side of St Paul's Cathedral, the City Information Centre is the primary source of tourist and visitor information for the City of London. Staff at the City Information Centre speak many languages and are knowledgeable about the City. Many leaflets, books and maps are available from the Centre.

London Stone

This ancient piece of limestone, now much reduced in size, was once a significant landmark in the City. Its origins and history are unknown, but much lore and myth are associated with it. The stone has been relocated several times and was until recently hidden almost out of sight behind a grille at street level in a shop front on Cannon Street. The stone clearly had great significance in times past as the first Mayor of London was Henry Fitzailwyn de Londenstone (Henry, son of Ailwyn, of the London Stone).

Dr Johnson's House

No. 17 Gough Square is one of several London properties that were lived in by Dr Samuel Johnson, famous for producing the first authoritative and comprehensive English dictionary in 1755. The house is doubly famous as the 'Blue Plaque' erected on the building was one of the first by the Royal Society of Arts, and it's not even blue! It is also the only circular 'Blue Plaque' in the City of London. Soon after the Blue Plaque scheme took off it was agreed that the Corporation of London would administer the scheme inside the Square Mile, whereas English Heritage now administers the scheme across the rest of London. City of London Blue Plaques have been rectangular ever since.

Tower Bridge

The iconic Tower Bridge lies fully outside the City of London limits and yet is owned and maintained by the City. This stems from the fact that the City commissioned the building of the bridge and the Bridge House Estates continue to fund its ongoing maintenance and operation.

The Monument

The 350th anniversary of the Great Fire of London was commemorated in 2016. The Monument to that momentous event was extensively refurbished in 2007-8 following a £4.5 million grant from the City of London Corporation. The Monument is open to the public throughout the year and accepts only cash payments.

In 1986 the Worshipful Company of Bakers accepted responsibility for the actions of one of its members, Thomas Faryner (sometimes Farriner), the King's Baker, who neglected to put out the fire in his ovens overnight thus causing the Great Fire of London in 1666. The Lord Mayor accepted the apology of the Master Baker and a plaque was unveiled at the location of Faryner's home and bakery on Pudding Lane. There was no mention of the Bakers' Company picking up the bill for the 13,200 homes, 89 churches and 44 Livery Halls that were destroyed during the fire.

Charterhouse

Although technically only one side of Charterhouse Square is in the City of London, Sutton's Hospital in Charterhouse has long been associated with the City since its founding in the early 17th century from the will of Thomas Sutton, Master of Ordnance in the North.

The alms house is home to 40 pensioners known as Brothers (Charterhouse admits men and women) many with professional connections to the City and Church. The first fruits of the mulberry trees in Charterhouse are by custom presented to the Lord Mayor. Residents must have limited financial means and have no living spouse or partner on admission to the Alms house.

Charterhouse was founded as both alms house and school, the latter moved to Godalming in Surrey in 1872. Among the last pupils to study at Charterhouse School when it was still co-located with the alms house was a young boy who later became Master of the Mercers' Company, Lord Robert Baden-Powell of Gilwell, founder of the World-Wide Scout Movement. Another famous pupil was William Makepeace Thackery.

Charterhouse runs regular weekday tours hosted by one of the Brothers. Details are available from their website. In 2017 Charterhouse opened an excellent museum in partnership with the Museum of London, entry is free. Charterhouse itself remains a living institution with a vital role in the modern world.

The Pattenmakers' Exhibition

This permanent little exhibition is in the Guild Church[5] of St Margaret Pattens on Rood Lane. A *patten* is a platform under the sole of a shoe to raise it from the mud. The exhibition features a

---

[5] A Guild Church is one established under the City of London (Guild Churches) Act of 1952. Such churches are not tied to a parish but serve the needs of the City's working population and other institutional parishioners such as Livery Companies.

wide range of artefacts associated with the craft of the Pattenmaker, including some medieval era pattens and the tools of the last working Pattenmaker purchased by the Company in 1903. Ladies are invited to remove their pattens before entering the church, and gentlemen are requested to wipe their shoes!

The Makers of Playing Cards 'Exhibition

This small but fascinating display tells the story of the Worshipful Company of Makers of Playing Cards and the development of the craft which regulated the import of cheap playing cards. The display is next to the entrance to the City of London Police Museum at Guildhall library.

The Clockmakers 'Museum

The extensive museum of the Worshipful Company of Clockmakers relocated from Guildhall to the Science Museum in Kensington in 2015. It is now an entire gallery featuring over 1000 watches, 80 clocks and 25 maritime chronometers including John Harrison's 5th model and a long-case clock made by Thomas Tompion, father of English clockmaking and Master of the Company in 1704.

The City of London Police Museum

Until recently this hidden City gem was housed in Wood Street Police Station and open only on selected weekdays. The City of London Police Museum has now relocated to Guildhall, adjacent to the library. This museum tells the story of the City's own Police Force, which has always been separate from the Metropolitan Police and remains so today. Full of exhibits and fascinating stories of crime and policing in the City, the museum is a popular destination in its new, more accessible, home that is open during business hours and from 10:00 - 16:00 on Saturday. Free entry.

Note: The City of London Police Museum has one of the last remaining City Police telephone boxes, which were omnipresent before the advent of personal radio transmitter/receivers. The light on top of the telephone box would be permanently lit when members of the Royal Family were in the City.

One of the few Public Call Boxes of the City of London Police that are still present in the City. This one is located in front of St Botolph without Aldgate. The phone is no longer operative.

The Coopers' Company Museum

The Worshipful Company of Coopers maintains a museum to the art and craft of cooperage (cask and barrel making) in their hall. An immense range of exhibits connected with the craft traces the history of the Company back to the 13th century. The museum is also home to many of the Company's treasures, important documents and artwork.

Note: The Coopers' Company Museum is open only by prior arrangement with the Clerk to the Company.

The Glaziers' Company Stained Glass Repository

The London Stained Glass Repository was set up in 1982 to rescue stained glass of artistic merit or historical interest in buildings that are under threat of closure, vandalism or demolition. The repository then works to re-home the glass in a suitable setting, which is usually a church. Most of the glass goes to buildings in the UK, although some has gone to the USA, Australia and even the Falkland Islands. While the repository is not open to the public, some of the glass may be viewed on the Stained-Glass Repository website.

The Company has contributed to, and continues to support and consult with, the Stained-Glass Museum in Ely Cathedral, Cambridgeshire.

The Roman Bath House

Located in the basement of an office complex on Lower Thames Street, the Billingsgate Roman Bath House dates from the 2nd century and was discovered in 1848 during construction work. The Bath House is open to pre-booked guided tours on most but not all Saturdays throughout the year (check in advance). Tour last 45 minutes and are led by City of London guides. Access to the Bath House is via a staircase inside an office complex. £10 (2019 prices)

Open House London

Some of the Livery halls open their doors to the public on Open House London weekend (usually the third weekend in September). Prior booking might be required or a guided tour might be available at fixed times. The halls are under no obligation to open their doors, and visiting arrangements can vary from year to year, so always check with the Open House London website to see which halls are planning to open. Details are usually available from mid-August and a guide is available to purchase. Entry is free to all Open House London buildings.

Pray in the City

I cannot think of any city more commendable for the habits of its citizens in attending church, in observing the divine festivals, in giving alms, in providing hospitality, in formalising betrothals, in contracting marriages, in celebrating weddings, as well as in attention to the burial and funeral needs of the deceased.

William Fitzstephen, late 12th Century

Many of the ancient Livery Companies were first established as religious fraternities in the early Middle Ages; they were seen as being full of worship(pers) and so termed 'worshipful'. These Guilds adopted a patron saint and provided for the mutual protection and spiritual well-being of their members. Associations with the church remained strong until the Reformation.

The connection between the Livery and religion is apparent in the formal name of some older Companies, for example the *Master and Wardens and Brethren and Sisters of the Guild or Fraternity of the Blessed Mary the Virgin of the Mistery of Drapers of the City of London.*

City Churches

At the Reformation there were 108 churches and chapels in the City. Surviving today, apart from St Paul's Cathedral, are 45 churches, of which 40 are Anglican, one United Reformed, one Dutch Reformed, one Welsh Presbyterian, one German Lutheran, and one Roman Catholic. There are also several ruined Churches, two Chapels, and a Synagogue, Bevis Marks, which is the oldest Jewish place of worship in Britain.

Although no longer in the City, St Mary Aldermanbury church, which was seriously damaged during the Second World War, was rebuilt in Fulton, Missouri and designated by Congress as the National Churchill Museum of the United States of America.

Churches in the City of London still have a strong connection with the Livery Companies and all Liverymen and Freemen of Guilds and Livery Companies should know their Company's associated Guild church (see Appendix F). The Friends of the City Churches provide a comprehensive guide to the churches in the City of London (details in the 'Online Resources' chapter) and there are several excellent guides to the City Churches (see Bibliography). The Friends also operate a membership scheme with annual and life membership categories.

A few examples among many:

Sir Christopher Wren built St Paul's Cathedral out of the ashes of the Great Fire of London. St Paul's is the seat of the Bishop of London and the final resting place of many national heroes including Admiral Lord Nelson. The Cathedral has also served as the focus for royal weddings and events of national thanksgiving and remembrance. The cathedral is 365 feet tall and was the tallest building in the City until 1962. Several cathedrals have stood on the site, with the earliest dating from around 886. The current building is the fifth St Paul's Cathedral in the City. Every year all the Livery Companies join with the Lord Mayor and other City officials for the United Guilds Service (see below).

St Lawrence Jewry sits in the southwest corner of Guildhall yard and is the Guild Church to the City of London Corporation. The church is one of Sir Christopher Wren's designs and dates from after the Great Fire of London in 1666. The weathervane of the church is a golden gridiron, symbol of St Lawrence who was roasted on a gridiron. The church is affiliated with the New Zealand Society UK and holds an annual Waitangi Day Service. The church is open from Monday to Friday, 08:00 - 18:00. Reverend Canon David Parrott has produced an updated version of the Rules for the Conduct of Life (based on the version handed to all newly admitted Freemen) and available from the church for £10 (2019 price).

Another City of London church designed by Sir Christopher Wren is St Benet Paul's Wharf on Queen Victoria Street. St Benet has been the church to HM College of Arms since 1555 and has the distinction of holding a regular Sunday service in Welsh with a translation for English speakers!

The Priory Church of St Bartholomew the Great in Smithfield holds the distinction of having a Norman-era interior that dates from as early as 1123 and has been used as a film set for many films and TV programmes. The church has been in constant use since 1143 and is now associated with at least seven Livery Companies. It claims to be the oldest church in the City.

The oldest religious foundation in the City is All Hallows by the Tower, which claims to have been founded in the year 675. The church is home to one of the City's lesser-known traditions, the Knollys Rose Ceremony, mentioned previously.

Corporation of London Benefices

The City of London Corporation is patron, either singularly or jointly with other organisations, of 10 benefices of the Church of England. This gives the Corporation the right of presentation (the nomination of the vicar or rector) to the following churches: Guild Church of St Lawrence Jewry, St Alban with St Augustine (Fulham), St John on Bethnal Green, St John the Evangelist (Brownswood Park), St Mark (Clerkenwell), St Mathias (Stoke Newington), St Peter-upon-Cornhill, St Peter with St Thomas (Bethnal Green), St George the Martyr (Southwark) and St John (North Woolwich).

Livery Company Benefices

In addition to the Corporation benefices, several Livery Companies are patrons, either singularly or jointly with other organisations, of benefices of the Church of England. Just a few example benefices are the Mercers' Company (8 benefices), the Grocers' Company (13 benefices), the Drapers' Company (1 benefice), the Haberdashers' Company (8 benefices), and the Merchant Taylors (1 benefice). The Mercers' Company is also the only Livery Company to have a Chapel in its hall.

The Spital Sermon

This ancient sermon has been preached since the late 14th century. The sermon takes its name from St Mary Spital - The Hospital of St Mary without Bishopsgate - a *spital* being a name for a place where the sick were cared for in medieval times. The sermon was once attended by the Lord Mayor, Aldermen and officials from various royal hospitals. In modern times the sermon is often given by a bishop at the invitation of the Lord Mayor and is held at St Lawrence Jewry, usually in February or March, on the same day as the meeting of the Court of Common Council.

Plough Monday Service at St Lawrence Jewry

This annual service, held early in January on the Monday after Epiphany (6th January), is attended by the Lord Mayor. Prayers are given for the staff and work of the Corporation of London. In 2010 the service was updated for the modern working environment; no ploughs are used in the City but smartphones and laptops were blessed for the first time as a new means by which God's grace may reach us all.

Stationers 'Ash Wednesday St Paul's Service with Cakes and Ale

Alderman John Norton, thrice Master of the Stationers' Company in the early 17th century, left a bequest for the Company to hold an annual Ash Wednesday sermon and that the members be provided with cakes and ale (and other victuals). The service is held at St Paul's Cathedral early in the afternoon on Ash Wednesday preceded by a Company lunch buffet in Stationers' Hall.

The Lion Sermon

Sir John Gayer (1646-47), Lord Mayor and founder of the Levant Company (trading with the Ottoman Empire), left a bequest to St Katharine Cree Church in gratitude for an incident during his travels in Syria when he came across a lion. He prayed for mercy and the lion departed doing him no harm. The sermon is given in the church each year at 13:00 on 16th October (or the nearest weekday) and has been a feature of the City calendar for over 370 years.

The Bubble Sermon

This is a closed sermon organised by The Worshipful Company of Stationers and Newspaper Makers. The sermon is held at St Bride's Church, Fleet Street on the first Tuesday in June with a reminder that 'Life is but a bubble'. The sermon is held in memory of Richard Johnson, a former member and benefactor of the Company. Attendance is only by invitation from a member of the Stationers' Company.

Musicians 'Company Choral Evensong

This event is open to the public and held annually, usually in October, at St Paul's Cathedral. The event is held in memory of St Cecilia, the Patron Saint of Music, and is organised by the Worshipful Company of Musicians. Featured in this service is the rarely heard 'Elegy for Strings' by Sir Edward Elgar, which he wrote in 1909 for the Musicians' Company. Its inclusion serves to remember those Company members who have died in the past year.

Festival of St Cecilia

This event, supported by the Musicians' Company Benevolent Fund, rotates annually between St Paul's Cathedral, Westminster Abbey and Westminster Cathedral on the Wednesday morning nearest to the feast day of St Cecilia on 22nd November. The service combines the choirs of all three institutions and is the only time they sing together. A new anthem is composed for the service each year. The Masters and Clerks of the Livery Companies attend wearing their robes and regalia. After the service a lunch is served and a notable figure in the arts world gives a speech.

Festival Service of the Sons and Friends of the Clergy

This event dates to 1655 and was originally founded to support the families of those clergy members who had remained loyal to the Crown during the English Civil War. Lord Protector Oliver Cromwell deprived those clergymen of their income, leaving their families destitute. The service continues to raise charitable funds for the clergy of the Anglican Communion and their families in times of financial distress. The service is held in May at St Paul's Cathedral.

The United Guilds 'Service

This is a relatively recent annual event by City standards. It was instituted during the dark days of the Second World War to show the solidarity of the City Livery Companies with the City's citizens. Every year, usually on the Friday two weeks before Good Friday, the Lord Mayor, Sheriffs, Aldermen and senior officers of the corporation along with all the Masters of the Livery Companies and 20 or so from each of their membership attend a Thanksgiving Service at St Paul's Cathedral.

This event affords the third occasion, along with the two meetings of Common Hall, to see the Masters of all the Livery Companies adorned in their ceremonial robes and to attend at St Paul's at full capacity. The Bishop of London together with the Master Mercer and Master Grocer formally welcome the Lord Mayor at the great West Doors, rarely opened otherwise. A senior church figure then preaches a sermon.

St Paul's Choristers

Several of the Livery Companies sponsor one or more of the choristers of the St Paul's Cathedral Choir. Each chorister receives a medallion, usually bearing the Company's insignia, on appointment, and wears it on special occasions. Sponsorship usually lasts a period of several years so the list of Companies who are sponsoring choristers tends to vary over time. An up-to-date list may always be found on the St Paul's Cathedral website.

Several Livery Companies have a choir. The Horners' Company Choir began in 1985 and now sings at the Company's annual carol service and at the annual election service at St James Garlickhythe. More recently the World Traders' Company and the Educators' Company have both formed choirs.

The Temple of Mithras

For those of a pre-Christian persuasion, the Temple of Mithras re-open in November 2017. Restored to its original location by Museum of London Archaeology (MOLA) with the support of Bloomberg L.P., the temple was discovered in 1954 and relocated from Walbrook Square to Temple Court on Queen Victoria Street to allow the building of Bucklersbury House. When Bloomberg purchased Walbrook Square it was announced the Temple would be restored to its original location, now some 21 feet below street level. The Temple is an example of a Mithraeum, dedicated to the mysterious Roman God Mithras and was a place of initiation and the location where secretive rituals were conducted.

City Courses, Briefings, Tours, Lectures, Libraries and History Societies

Livery Committee Courses

The Livery Committee organises courses and briefings for new Freemen, Liverymen, Livery Company Masters, Wardens, Court Assistants and Clerks. Of note is the regular City Briefing that provides an overview of the City and the Livery Companies. The City Briefing is ideally suited to prospective or recently admitted Freemen or Liverymen who wish to learn more about the City and its link with Livery Companies. Briefings take place on weekday evenings at Guildhall, usually starting at 17:30 and finishing by 19:00. A drinks reception follows the briefing. Further details are in the Online Resources chapter. Cost £20 (2019 rates).

Gresham College Lectures

Gresham College is a City institution and London's oldest university, founded by Sir Thomas Gresham, a Mercer, under his will of 1573. The College, which the City of London and the Mercers support through their joint ownership of the Royal Exchange, runs a series of free public lectures on a wide range of topics.

The College also provides on its website near-simultaneous online transmission, and audio and video recording of many past lectures with transcripts and presentation slides. Lectures are usually given in the Museum of London or in the College itself at Barnard's Inn.

Note: Barnard's Inn has a small capacity, and popular lectures can become crowded, so it is best to arrive early to secure a seat.

Some of the more notable lectures on the City, Freedom and Livery recorded by Gresham College and available for download or viewing online are as follows:

- *City of London Livery Companies* by Professor Tim Connell
- *Freedom of the City of London (Sheep across London Bridge)* by Murray D Craig
- *What has the City (of London) ever done for us?* By Alderman Sir David Wootton (Lord Mayor 2011-12)
- *The History of the Lord Mayor's Show* by Dominic Reid OBE (Pageantmaster)
- *The Governance and Voting System of the City of* London by Tony Travers
- *The Livery Companies in Tudor* London by Professor Tim Connell
- *800 Years of the Lord Mayor's Show* by Dominic Reid OBE (Pageantmaster), Tracey Hill and Robert Green
- *Envy of Kings: The Guildhall of London and the Power of the Medieval Corporation* by Dr Simon Thurley
- *The City of London and the Magna Carta* by Anthony Arlidge QC

Since 2009 the College has hosted an annual 'Lord Mayor's Lecture'. Attendance is free at this or any other lecture hosted by Gresham College. Booking is essential, and tickets are available from Gresham College. Some of the Gresham College lectures take place in the Museum of London, which has greater capacity.

Stephen Fry's 'Keys to the City'

On his being admitted into the Freedom of the City of London, the actor Stephen Fry recorded a television documentary about the City's unique status in Britain. Titled 'Keys to the City', it offers a quick and easily digestible tour around some of the City's civic and commercial institutions, ceremonies and customs. The documentary is available on the world wide web.

Secret City of London Videos

C.G.P Grey has created two excellent short introductions to the City of London that are available on YouTube:

- *The Secret City of London, Part 1: History* - giving a condensed summary of the history of the City
- *The Secret City of London, Part 2: Government* - providing an overview of the City's unique voting system

Together they provide a tempting *amuse-bouche* to this trencherman's guide to the City, Freedom and Livery.

Points of clarification on the Secret City of London videos:

- These video clips give a hint of implied mutual distrust between the City and the Crown. If ever this was true it hasn't been so for over 200 years, with senior members of the Royal Family being active members of City Livery Companies (see the chapter 'Royal Connections').
- The Liverymen also approve the candidates for Lord Mayor before the Aldermen make their selection.
- It is also possible to stand for election to Common Council as the nominated representative of a Livery Company.
- As a practical matter, all Aldermen and Lord Mayors of London are members of at least one, if not multiple Livery Companies.

Guildhall Library and City Business Library

Located in the Guildhall complex, Guildhall Library is a public reference library open from Monday to Saturday. The library specialises in the history of London and also houses the libraries of several Livery Companies and of Gresham College.

The Library is the venue for a series of exhibitions and regular public talks on a wide range of subjects usually related to City history, literature, art and the Livery Companies. Many of these exhibitions and talks are free to attend.

The Library also sells a range of books and maps related to the City of London (including this guide and the associated posters).

Co-located with the Guildhall Library, the City Business Library (CBL) specialises in supporting the needs of small and medium enterprises. CBL provides access to an immense array of business databases and has a team of expert staff focused on the needs of small businesses, entrepreneurs, charities and social enterprises. It also has a range of meeting and training rooms available for hire at modest costs.

The London Metropolitan Archives (LMA)

The LMA is the document archive for the City of London and access is provided free of charge. The archives hold a comprehensive collection of prints, drawings, maps, plans and photographs relating to London. The archive also provides an online catalogue (see the chapter 'Online Resources') and a library specialising in the history of London. The LMA runs regular exhibitions and provides support for educational institutions.

The Guildhall Historical Association

This rather exclusive group was formed in 1944 and was a well-kept secret until recently. Membership is by invitation only, and its purpose is to 'collect, publish and preserve material of historical interest connected with the City'. Published papers dating back to 1944 are now freely available on the Association's website covering topics as diverse as the wine trade and the City of London, the office of the Recorder of the City of London, and city banqueting. The papers published by the Association are a treasure trove for research on a wide range of City topics.

The City of London Historical Society

Rather less exclusive is this society formed circa 1980 to foster and promote interest in the Square Mile. The society meets regularly for walks, talks, tours and behind-the-scenes visits to places of interest in the City. The Society is a membership organisation, the annual subscription is just £10 (2019 rate).

The Friends of Guildhall Art Gallery

The Guildhall Art Gallery operates a 'Friends' scheme where, for a modest subscription, Friends gain access to previews and private viewings in addition to free entrance to exhibitions and to Keats House, Tower Bridge and the Monument. Friends also receive a regular newsletter and discounts at the Guildhall Art Gallery and Guildhall Library shops.

City of London Guided Walks

The City of London has its own Guide Lecturers' Association and a rigorous qualification for tour guides specialising in the Square Mile. The City Guides offer a selection of regular walks and tours on various City themes, including:

- Guildhall Art Gallery and Roman London's Amphitheatre
- The Mansion House
- Smithfield Market
- Guildhall
- City Highlights - the top ten sights
- City Gardens
- Roman London
- St Bartholomew's Hospital
- The Roman Bath House (Billingsgate)

In addition to these regular walking tours, City Guides offer a wealth of tours on both general City history and special interest tours covering aspects of the City.

Of particular note are the free tours offered by City Guides during the afternoon following the Lord Mayor's Show. Walking tours commence at 3pm and leave from No. 1 Poultry at regular intervals until 4pm. There is no need to book in advance and a donation to the Lord Mayor's Appeal is appreciated.

Eat, Drink and Sleep in the City

The City is well served with cafés, restaurants, pubs and hotels. Various lesser-known events and venues are also available to Freemen and Liverymen.

The Mercers' Company owns and operates No. 6 Frederick's Place, a grade II listed Georgian era town house, which provides nine bedrooms for members of Livery Companies. The house was built by the Adam brothers (Robert and James) in the 1770s and was once the office of Benjamin Disraeli. A self-service breakfast is included. Rooms are available Monday-Saturday, booking via bedrooms@mercers.co.uk. A note from your Livery Company's Clerk or Beadle will be required to confirm your company membership at the time of booking.

No. 6 Frederick's Place, Georgian era elegance in the City

The Vintners' Company Hall provides accommodation at modest rates for Freemen, Liverymen and their guests who wish to stay overnight in the City. Some of the bedrooms are en-suite, while others use washing facilities shared among guests. Details are available from the Vintners' Company website.

Guildhall has single and double bedrooms that are available to Masters (or Deputising Past Masters) and Clerks of City Livery Companies on a pre-booked basis when attending City functions. Details are available from Guildhall.

The Little Ship Club has single and double-berth 'cabins' available to members of the Club.

The Butchers' Company hosts a regular monthly lunchtime carvery in its hall every month except August and excluding the Christmas and New Year period. The carvery is open to Freemen of the City of London and Liverymen of all City Livery Companies. Lunch is 12:30 arrival for 13:00 seated.

The Ironmongers' Hall hosts a lunch every Monday between noon and 14:00. It is open to members of all the Livery Companies and their guests. Lunches are not served in August or on bank holiday Mondays.

The Master Mariners' Company hosts a monthly curry lunch open to all Liverymen of that Company and their guests. Bookings may be made through the Clerk to the Master Mariners' Company.

Watermen's Hall is the venue for the monthly River Thames Lunch Club, which is open to the public and is usually held on the second Friday of each month. Details may be found on the Company's website.

Café Below is in the undercroft of St Mary-le-Bow on Cheapside. It is a family-run enterprise, which every Cockney should visit as St Mary-le-Bow is the home of Bow Bells.

Life's Kitchen, in association with various wine merchants, hosts Livery Wine and Dine events three times a year at various Livery halls in the City. Reception is at 18:45, dinner at 19:30.

The Barbican Conservatory (open to the public Sunday afternoons and some Bank Holiday Mondays) spans over 23,000 square feet and is home to some 2,000 tropical plants, fish and terrapins. It offers afternoon tea for pre-booked groups of 6 or more on some Sundays (check Barbican website). These afternoon teas book up quickly despite being almost unknown outside the residents of the Barbican estate.

The Guildhall Yard hosts a Lunch Market on the same days that the Court of Common Council meets. The market features over 20 stalls serving food from around the world.

The annual City Beerfest is held in early July in Guildhall Yard. This event is jointly organised by the Worshipful Company of Brewers and the City Music Foundation. A wide range of craft brewers set up their pavilions in the market, complemented by food stalls and entertained by various bands. All proceeds go to the Lord Mayor's Appeal and the City Music Foundation.

The City of London Distillery (Bride Lane) was unique among commercial organisations in the City in being permitted to use the City's coat of arms on its signage and range of gin bottles for some years. The bottles are a work of art that echo the dome of St Paul's Cathedral. The distillery's gins are aptly named: Square Mile, Christopher Wren, City of London and so on. Organised tours of the distillery are available, as is a gin lab experience during which one may distil one's own unique blend of gin.

The Middle Temple offers lunch to non-members in the magnificent surroundings of the tudor hall, on weekdays during legal term time. Non-members must book in advance and adhere to the dress code. Lunch may also be combined with a group tour of the Temple, again booked in advance.

Most of the Livery Company Halls[6] are available for private hire for business and social events. Many of the Livery Companies have tied caterers drawn from select well-established and reliable City catering businesses. Each hall has its own unique character and capacities vary from 30 - 300 depending on the venue.

---

[6] The Fishmongers' Company produced a guide to cooking a wide range of fish and chip dishes to celebrate the 150th anniversary of fish and chips in 2010.

Livery Company Sport and Social Events

Many of the City Livery Companies have their own sporting and social groups hosting regular events and competitions for company members. Some events operate across the Livery Companies and have developed into annual fixtures.

The better-established events are as follows:

Clay Pigeon Shooting

This event is organised by the Worshipful Company of Environmental Cleaners, usually in May. Whilst the day has a competitive element, it is essentially a charity fund-raising event and is held at the Holland & Holland shooting ground in Northwood, Middlesex.

Bridge Competition

Aptly, this event is organised and subsidised by the Worshipful Company of Makers of Playing Cards. It is held on the first Monday of March at Drapers' Hall. Only members of Livery Companies are permitted to enter the competition.

Prince Arthur of Connaught Golf Tournament

Probably the most prestigious sporting event in the Livery Company calendar, this event is organised by the Worshipful Company of Coachmakers and Coach Harness Makers. It recalls the admission of HRH Prince Arthur of Connaught to the Company in 1927. The competition is now held annually in May at Walton Heath, Surrey.

Croquet Tournament

The Worshipful Company of Founders organises an annual croquet tournament, which is held at Surbiton Croquet Club. Prizes are awarded, including a wooden spoon!

Tennis Tournament

The Worshipful Company of Feltmakers organises the annual Inter-Livery Tennis Competition, which is usually held at Queen's Club in September.

Skiing Competition

This annual event is organised by the Worshipful Company of Ironmongers and held at Morzine in France during January. Livery Companies may send teams of three or four who may be Freemen, Liverymen, Apprentices or Journeymen.

Sailing Events

The City Livery Yacht Club is the focus for several sailing events including the annual Lord Mayor's Cup organised by the Royal Corinthian Yacht Club in Cowes.

Young Inter-Livery Events

The Pewterers' Company organises an extensive calendar of Young Inter-Livery events for Freemen and Liverymen in the (approximately) 20 - 40 age range. Past events include an Agatha Christie-themed evening, a Spring 'Dinner and Dance', an Inter-Livery Quiz Night and a Night of Magic and Mystery.

Swimathon

Organised by the Chartered Surveyors' Company as a fun, friendly swimming relay to raise charity funds, the swimathon has mixed-ability swimming teams participating in a 5 km challenge over 2.5 hours. It is held at the RAC Club in Epsom.

Brigantes - Liverymen in the North

The first Brigantes event was held in Manchester during May 2015 for Liverymen living beyond reasonable commuting distance to London. The intention is to provide an opportunity for social interaction among the Livery and to strengthen Livery Company links with members in the north of England, which is defined as Leicester to the Scottish boarder.

So successful was the first event that further dates were soon announced including one at the Cutlers' Hall in Hallamshire (a provincial Guild with links to the City of London Livery Companies) which the author was pleased to attend.

The Brigantes were an ancient Celtic tribe in the north of England and the Brigantes Breakfast has adopted a quasi-Celtic knot device as its branding with the Yorkist and Lancastrian colours of red and white respectively.

It seems certain that this new forum for Liverymen in the north of England will flourish 'root and branch'. For further details of events contact livery@brigantes.org.uk

The Brigantes brand identity, reproduced with courtesy of the Brigantes event committee.

City Clubs, Societies and Associations

The Guild of Young Freemen

Founded by the City of London Corporation in 1976 to encourage involvement of younger Freemen and Liverymen with the affairs and traditions of the City, the Guild is aimed at Freemen and Liverymen under the age of 40, whether or not members of a Livery Company. The society offers an extensive programme of annual events. It has the Lord Mayor as its patron. In May 2016 a grand banquet was held at Mansion House to mark the 40th anniversary of the Guild, to which all Freemen of the City of London under the age of 45 were invited.

The Guild of Freemen of the City of London

This Guild is open to all Freemen of the City of London, whether or not members of a Livery Company. Formed in 1908, the Guild has a similar structure to a Livery Company but without the trade, craft or professional association, and with a membership limit of 3,500. The Guild operates a full calendar of social and charitable events. Long-standing members of the Guild of Young Freemen are exempt from the joining fee. The Guild has the Lord Mayor as its patron and the Dean of St Paul's is the Honorary Chaplain.

The City Livery Club

The City Livery Club, founded in 1914, is a private members' club for Liverymen of the Livery Companies and the two established City Companies without Livery (Watermen and Lightermen, and Parish Clerks). Freemen of the City of London and members of City of London Guilds, other City Companies without Livery, the Royal Society of St George (City Branch), the Ward Clubs, the Guildable Manor of Southwark and the Institute of Directors (City Branch) may join as associate members, all of whom enjoy membership benefits without rights to vote or to become officers of the club.

The club is privileged to count the Right Honourable The Lord Mayor as Patron and Member. The club provides a City venue where members can meet, dine and exchange views in comfortable premises shared with the Little Ship Club.

The club also provides a broad programme of events, both formal and informal, with various interests represented by Sections for History and Antiques, Investments, Motoring, Music, Wine, Golf, Tennis, Aeronautics, Photography, and Women in the Livery. The club has reciprocal arrangements with many other clubs in the UK and abroad.

In 2014 the City Livery Club celebrated its centenary by instituting a new award, the Root and Branch Award, to recognise an individual Liveryman (or group of Liverymen) who made an exceptional contribution to the work of their Livery Company or the wider body of the Livery. The first winner of the Root and Branch Award was Tom Ilube CBE (Information Technologist) and a special one-off lifetime award was made to Geoffrey Bond OBE, Past Master of the Glaziers' Company. In 2016 the Root and Branch Award was presented to the author of this guide for his work in promoting the City and its Livery Companies. Details other award winners may be found in the appendices.

Past Masters 'Associations

Except for the Bowyers' Company, whose Master is elected for two years, each Livery Company elects a new Master annually. The Masters of the various Companies naturally meet at events during their year in office. In order to maintain contact and fellowship, a Past Masters' Association is usually formed to include all the Masters from a given year. The associations go by curious titles such as Temple Bar Masters, Trafalgar 200 Masters, and After Eight Masters. There is also a single association for all lady Masters and Past Masters, the latter are also members of the Past Masters' Association for their year.

A full list is in the City of London Directory and Livery Companies Guide (see bibliography).

City Consorts Society

This society, formed in 2017, aims to support the consorts of Livery Company Masters and those of the Senior Wardens as they approach their year in office. The City Consorts Society runs events, provides advice and guidance to consorts, and acts as a communication channel between current and forthcoming consorts to aid their enjoyment and engagement with the myriad activities of the Master's year.

The Clerks 'Associations

The Clerks to each of the Livery Companies have their own associations that play a vital role in inter-Livery coordination, not to mention competitiveness. There are three associations for Clerks: The Great Twelve (only for the Clerks to the XII); The Association of Clerks for those Companies, except the XII and certain others, that have a hall which the Company owns and not the Company's charity (hence some Companies with halls are not eligible); and finally The Fellowship of Clerks, which is open to all Clerks.

Each of the three Clerks' Associations elects two of their members to the City's Livery Committee (six in total).

The (Livery) Beadles 'Guild

Each City Livery Company appoints a Beadle, who is Master of Ceremonies and Toastmaster for the Company. The Beadle holds the Company Stave and leads the Company's Master and Wardens at social and civic ceremonial events. Each Ward of the City of London also elects a Ward Beadle, who has certain civic and ceremonial roles supporting the Ward Alderman. The Beadles' Guild brings together the Livery Company and Ward Beadles in a fraternity much like a City Company without Livery.

The City of London Ward Beadles

The City of London Ward Beadles' Association was founded in 1895 and represents their interests with the Corporation. It includes currently serving and retired Ward Beadles. The Court of Aldermen recognises the association, which various City officers consult on ceremonial and security matters.

The City of London Sheriffs' Society

The first meeting of this rather select Society was held in November of 1956, although discussion about forming a society for the City's Sheriffs (past and present) began in 1953. The Society brings together all current and former Sheriffs which will of course includes all late Lord Mayors. A book on the history of the Society was published in 2023 but is not available commercially (see bibliography). It should be noted that the office of Sheriff predates that of the Lord Mayor by many centuries.

The Ward Clubs

The 25 Wards of the City of London each have a Ward Club (some Wards share a club). The Ward Clubs are primarily social clubs aimed at residents and those who work in the City, particularly the business voters. The Ward Clubs also provide another link between the electorate and the Court of Common Council, since the Aldermen and Common Councilmen are invariably members of the club for their ward. The Ward Clubs are the body that organises the Wardmote (Ward Moot) at which candidates for election to the office of Common Councilman or Alderman are elected. The Ward Beadle opens and closes the Wardmote and in times past would have fined Freemen who failed to attend.

Also, a United Wards' Club provides a social club for the whole City and runs an extensive programme of educational, social and sporting events.

The Wards of the City of London are:

Aldersgate	Dowgate
Aldgate	Farringdon Within
Bassishaw	Farringdon Without
Billingsgate	Langbourn
Bishopsgate	Lime Street
Bread Street	Portsoken
Bridge	Queenhithe
Broad Street	Tower
Candlewick	Vintry
Castle Baynard	Walbrook
Cheap	
Coleman Street	Note: Lime Street and Cornhill share a Ward Club, as do Vintry and Dowgate, and the two Farringdon Wards.
Cordwainer	
Cornhill	
Cripplegate	

City Branches of Other Institutions

Various charities and other organisations have an active "City Branch". Some examples are as follows:

- Institute of Directors
- Red Cross
- Royal National Lifeboat Institution
- Royal Society of St George
- Royal Marine Association
- Salvation Army (International Headquarters)
- Royal Humane Society (Headquarters)
- Many masonic lodges in addition to those listed in Appendix A.

Several other ancient and noble City clubs and societies, in rude health and counting many City dignitaries and Liverymen among their membership, have chosen to remain beyond the purview of this comprehensive guide.

City Livery Yacht Club

There can be no mystery about the purpose of this club. Membership is open to Freemen and Liverymen of City Livery Companies who like messing about in boats. Originally part of the City Livery Club, it was recognised in 1958 by the Royal Yachting Association as a yacht club.

The Thames Traditional Rowing Association (TTRA)

The TTRA was founded in 2003 and supports the sport of fixed seat rowing and sculling on the Thames. The Association counts a growing number of Livery Companies among its membership (see Appendix H). Each Company appoints a Bargemaster, who is usually a Freeman of the Watermen and Lightermen's Company. The TTRA members participate in many events including the Lord Mayor's River Progress, The Tudor Pull and

The Port of London Challenge. In 2014 the TTRA was granted armorial bearings in recognition of its role.

The City of London Piscatorial Society

A fancy name for one of the UK's oldest angling clubs, The City of London Piscatorial Society, founded in 1902, has a closed membership and usually has a waiting list for new members. The club owns three fisheries in south-east England on the River Loddon near Wargrave, on the River Colnbrook near Wraysbury, and on Wayside Lake near Woking.

The City of London Bowling Club

The game of Lawn Bowls is first recorded by William Fitzstephen in 12th century London. How appropriate then that the game continues in the City. The City of London Bowling Club is a venerable City institution, founded in 1924. Its home is Finsbury Circus, London's oldest public park. The Club boasts an immaculate bowling green and smart pavilion (dating from 1968). The Lord Mayor is President of the Club.

The Portsoken Volunteers

This military re-enactment society is based on the original volunteer unit formed in 1798 as a sort of Home Guard for the City during the Napoleonic era. It now parades at the Red Feather Day ceremony, the annual beating of the bounds of St Botolph without Aldgate and occasionally in the Lord Mayor's Show.

Other Notable City Institutions

London, thou art of towns A per se.
  Sovereign of cities, seemliest in sight,
Of high renown, riches and royalty;
  Of lords, barons, and many a goodly knight;
  Of most delectable lusty ladies bright;
Of famous prelates, in habits clerical;
  Of merchants full of substance and of might:
London, thou art the flower of Cities all.

William Dunbar, In Honour of the City of London, early 16th century

The Central Criminal Court

The Central Criminal Court, commonly known as the Old Bailey, is certainly the best-known crown court in the United Kingdom if not in the world. The Old Bailey is a centre of excellence for trying some of the most serious crimes of terrorism, murder, and serious sex offences, and would presumably handle any trial for treason.

Although it is a national institution, it is owned, administered and protected by the City Corporation. The Old Bailey is unique in this respect, being the only Crown Court not owned and operated by the Ministry of Justice.

The central seat in each of the court rooms at the Old Bailey is reserved for the exclusive use of The Lord Mayor, who takes precedence over all the judges. The Lord Mayor opens the new court session up to four times a year in full ceremonial dress, accompanied by the City Marshal, Common Cryer and Sergeant-at-Arms, the Sheriffs and the Secondary of London and Under Sheriff. This is the only occasion when the ceremonial entrance gates to the Old Bailey are opened other than for visiting members of the Royal Family.

The court is on the site of the medieval Newgate Prison and is named after the City's defensive wall or 'Bailey', part of which is still visible in the basement. The Sheriffs of the City of London remain in residence during their year in office and use apartments provided at the Old Bailey complex for that purpose. The Sheriffs have access to a chauffeur and a maroon-coloured private London taxi that is emblazoned with the City of London's coat of arms. When the taxi isn't quite grand enough, each has a Rolls Royce Phantom VI and they are garaged at the Old Bailey. These latter vehicles fly the Lord Mayor's flag of office, which combines the City's flag with the City's coat of arms in the centre.

One of the two Sheriffs is on duty every day that the Courts are sitting together with a duty Alderman and hosts a lunch for the judges with three or four 'interesting' invited guests every day so that the judges may meet a wide cross-section from the Livery Companies, the City and business. As Liverymen progress to senior office, they may be invited to attend one of these lunches, after which they are invariably invited to sit in on a trial that has reached an important phase.

The judges' dining room is adorned with a display of heraldic shields of the coats of arms of Sheriffs of the City of London dating back to 1905 - exceptionally recent for an office that is recorded as long ago as the 7th century. The Royal Warrants of appointment for the incumbent Sheriffs are also on display at the entrance to the dining room.

Other City Courts

Apart from the Old Bailey, the City has its own Magistrates' Court, which was originally in the undercroft of Mansion House, but now resides across the street on Walbrook. At Guildhall Yard is the Mayor's and City of London Court (the civil or County Court of the City) and it is the only County Court in the United Kingdom that does not have the word *county* in its title. The Mayor's and City of London Court is unusual in having almost unlimited civil jurisdiction within the City. It is also the oldest civil court in the UK, dating from the late 13th century.

The City is also home to the Chancery Division of the High Court of Justice and two specialist courts, specifically the Technology & Construction Court and the Admiralty & Commercial Court, both in the Rolls Building.

Lastly and usually overlooked is the Earl Marshal's High Court of Chivalry, located within the College of Arms. This court last sat in 1954, although several armigerous organisations have threatened legal action against persons or organisations misappropriating their arms, a recent (2012) example being Aberystwyth Town Council's pursuit of a social media page that used the Council's arms without sanction. Fortunately, the matter was settled before it reached the Earl Marshal's court. Within the Court may be seen the purple velvet cushion on which Queen Elizabeth II sat during her coronation in 1953.

At the time of writing a new court complex has been announced by the City of London Corporation and the Ministry of Justice. Eighteen new court rooms will be available in a new building in on Fleet Street. This court will specialise in economic crime, fraud and IT based crime.

Every day people walk past HM College of Arms on Queen Victoria Street unaware that this is the home of English, Welsh, Northern Irish and most Commonwealth heraldry.

HM College of Arms

The College of Arms is part of the Royal Household and the official repository of coats of arms and pedigrees of English[7], Welsh, Northern Irish and Commonwealth families and their descendants. Headed by the grandly titled Garter Principal King of Arms, and supported by two provincial Kings of Arms, six Heralds and four Pursuivants, the work of the College is overseen by the hereditary Earl Marshal, the Duke of Norfolk. The College grants arms to eminent persons and corporate bodies, including the Livery Companies and many of their members. The College is also the location of the High Court of Chivalry which last sat in 1954. The City's ongoing relationship with the fascinating subject of heraldry is explored more fully later in this guide.

---

[7] Scotland has its own heraldic authority in the Court of Lord Lyon in Edinburgh.

Pikemen of the HAC's Company of Pikemen and Musketeers, bodyguard to the Lord Mayor and formed by Royal Warrant.

The Honourable Artillery Company (HAC)

The HAC is the oldest regiment in the UK and the second oldest in the world after the Vatican's Swiss Guard. They are the second most senior regiment in the British Army Reserve, a fact that every Sapper should know, with only the Royal Monmouthshire Royal Engineers (Militia) being more senior. Jerseymen may argue that the Royal Militia of the Island of Jersey is older still (formed in 1337), but that Army Reserve unit was mothballed for some years and existed as a Cadet Forces unit for a period.

Originally formed as a Guild with a Royal Charter dating from 1537, the HAC still has a similar structure to a Livery Company. The Aldermen of the City of London are all honorary members of the Company's Court.

It was formerly required for prospective HAC members to be Freemen of the City of London.

The Arms of the Honourable Artillery Company and their motto 'Armed Strength for Peace'

The HAC's Company of Pikemen and Musketeers is formed of veteran members of the HAC Regiment. The Pikemen and Musketeers form the Lord Mayor's bodyguard and may be seen every year in the Lord Mayor's Show when they provide an escort to the Lord Mayor's coach.

The HAC has another ceremonial unit, the Light Cavalry HAC, dating from 1861. The Light Cavalry was re-formed in 1979 as an escort to the Lady Mayoress. Membership of the Light Cavalry HAC is open to retired members of HM Armed Forces (regular or reserve) on recommendation by current members of the Company. Despite the name the Light Cavalry usually parades dismounted, although it often provides a small, mounted contingent in the Lord Mayor's Show.

Ancient and Honorable Artillery Company (AHAC)

Several early colonists of North America were former HAC members and formed The Ancient and Honorable Artillery Company of Massachusetts in 1638. The two organisations share a close bond and organise regular exchange visits.

The AHAC was founded on the model of London's HAC. The Company is based in Faneuil Hall in Boston which has been its headquarters since 1746. Visitors to Armoury House, home of the HAC in London, may note that the Stars and Stripes is on display in the dining room.

City of London Police Officers and their patrol cars at Guildhall Yard.

The City of London Police

The City of London has its own Police Force formed in 1839. The local Police Authority is the Court of Common Council; hence the City does not have a Police and Crime Commissioner as other counties and cities do. The City of London Police is recognised nationally as a centre of excellence for detection of economic crime.

The City of London Police has a curious connection with the Honourable Artillery Company, which despite being a military organisation also has a detachment of Special Constables who are part of the City of London Special Constabulary. The detachment is administered from the HAC's barracks at Armoury House. These Special Constables are civilian police officers and volunteers, and qualify to become members of the HAC Regiment. The HAC Special Constabulary was formed in 1919 and initially comprised veterans from the First World War.

City Police officers may be easily recognised by their crested custody helmets or red and white hatching on peaked caps. Unique among British police forces they have gold buttons and badges of rank. City Police officers wear a gold *aiguillette*[8] with No. 1 dress for ceremonial events. Senior officers wear the aiguillette on the right side, while lower-ranking officers wear it

---

[8] A series of ornamental braided loops with tapering ends that are worn over and under the shoulder.

on the left. Male sergeants and PCs wear a red and white striped 'duty band' on their sleeve for ceremonial occasions, believed to be the last police force in the UK to do so.

The Corporation of Trinity House

The Master, Wardens and Assistants of the Guild, Fraternity or Brotherhood of the most glorious and undivided Trinity, and of St. Clement in the Parish of Deptford-Strond were granted a Royal Charter by Henry VIII in 1514.

Trinity House is responsible for the lighthouses, light vessels, buoys and navigation beacons around England, Wales, Gibraltar (the most southerly of the Trinity House lighthouses is on Europa Point) and the Channel Islands. It is also the UK's largest-endowed maritime charity, wholly funded by its endowments, spending around £4 million each year on its charitable activities including the welfare of mariners, education and training, and the promotion of safety at sea. It is also a Deep-Sea Pilotage Authority. A Court of Elder Brethren, a Master and Deputy Master govern Trinity House. The current Master is HRH The Princess Royal.

The Bank of England

'The Old Lady of Threadneedle Street' was founded in 1694 in Mercers' Hall. After six months it relocated to Grocers' Hall where it remained for the next 40 years. Its first governor, Sir John Houblon, himself a Past Master of the Grocers' Company, became Lord Mayor of London in 1695. The Bank, which is on the site of his house, has a museum that is open to the public Monday to Friday, 10:00 - 17:00, and on the day of the Lord Mayor's Show and during Open House London weekend. Free entry.

Following the events of the Gordon riots in 1780, a detachment of Foot Guards mounted guard every night at the Bank of England. This guard was known as the Bank of England Picquet and was the only guard duty where the guardsmen were issued with plimsoles; the officer on duty was given half a bottle of port and permitted to bring 'one or two guests' to dinner. The Bank of England Picquet ceased in 1973 as modern security arrangements made a military guard unnecessary.

Friends of the HQS Wellington Trust

Headquarters ship, Wellington, is a *sloop* (a one-masted sailing boat) moored alongside the Embankment; it is the former hall of the Master Mariners' Company. The ship is named after the capital of New Zealand, which was her patrol station in the late 1930s. The HQS Wellington Trust supports the upkeep of the ship and operates a Friends scheme with various levels of membership granting access to lecture evenings, the ship's bar, an annual reception and more.

The Guildable Manor of Southwark

Parts of Southwark have been subject to the City's authority since the medieval period. The City desired control of the south side of London Bridge, the sole river crossing until 1750, to hold legal jurisdiction of miscreants and stymie the development of a competitor township. Edward III granted the 'Town of Southwark' alias the 'Guildable Manor' to the City in 1327. This required a Quit Rent to be paid 'forever to our Exchequer' by the City. This is still rendered at an annual ceremony presided over by the King's Remembrancer at the Exchequer Court.

The Guildable Manor is a territorial rather than trade, craft or profession-based association and comprises Juror Freemen of the Court Leet (a manorial court). The City acquired two other Southwark manors (the King's Manor and Great Liberty) from Edward VI in 1550. These three formed the Ward of Bridge

Without (outside the Roman Walls), also called 'The Town and Borough of Southwark'. The Court of Aldermen appointed its Alderman; there were no Common Councilmen. In 1978 the Bridge Within Ward of the City was merged with Bridge Without Ward to become the 'Ward of Bridge and Bridge Without'.

The Recorder of London as 'High Steward of Southwark' and the Under Sheriff as 'High Bailiff of Southwark' still summon the Courts of the three manors and swear in their Foremen and Officers annually, being the only bodies sworn in directly by the City, unlike the Livery which do so for themselves.

The City University

Recently ranked in the top five per cent of universities in the world and among the top 30 higher education institutions in the UK, City University has as its Rector the Right Honourable the Lord Mayor of London. Originally named the Northampton Institute after one of its founder benefactors, The Marquess of Northampton, City University received its Royal Charter in 1966. Since 2001 City University has incorporated the Inns of Court School of Law, which was established in 1852.

The City & Guilds of London Institute

Founded in 1878 by sixteen Livery Companies, this awarding body for trade, craft and professional qualifications was established by a group of 16 City Livery Companies. City & Guilds is now recognised worldwide as one of the premier qualification-awarding bodies for technical and vocational training and certification. The City & Guilds received their Royal Charter in 1900 and the Institute's President is HRH The Princess Royal.

The City & Guilds of London was founded at a time when the Livery Companies were under public scrutiny and their traditional role in regulating trade had almost disappeared. The

Livery Companies turned to their early roots as establishments for training apprentices in various crafts, trades and professions. They established a central examining body and a series of technical qualifications initially titled the *City and Guilds of London Institute for the Advancement of Technical Education*. Today some two million students in 81 countries and 8,500 colleges follow a range of around 500 courses to achieve City & Guilds qualifications. The Livery Companies still provide substantial support to this work.

The Honourable The Irish Society

The Irish Society is a charity that works for the benefit of the community in County Londonderry. The Society was created by Royal Charter in 1613 to undertake the plantation in the northwest of Ulster. At the time King James I thought the City of London the best organisation to fund, build and manage the rebuilding of the City of Derry, subsequently renamed Londonderry. The arms of the City of London are in chief (the upper third) of the arms of Londonderry differenced with a golden harp in the centre of the cross.

Nowadays The Irish Society uses income from properties it owns in Londonderry and Coleraine and various fishing rights on the rivers Bann and Foyle for charitable purposes in County Londonderry. The city walls of Londonderry are still owned by The Irish Society; the 12 cannons mounted at points along the wall were provided by the City of London (five) and various Livery Companies (seven). The Mayors of Londonderry and Coleraine serve on the advisory committee of The Irish Society. The governance court comprises Aldermen and Common Councilmen.

Note: A Past Lord Mayor occupies the role of Governor and is traditionally known as the Vice Admiral of the Northern Waters. A Deputy Governor is drawn from among the Common Councilmen.

The Honourable Company of Freemen of the City of London of North America

Formed in 1979, this Company brings together Freemen of the City of London who are resident in North America. The Company offers various grades of membership, with full members needing to be both Freemen and resident in North America. The Company elects a Master each year, and often they are also members of one of the City of London Livery Companies. In 2012 the then Lord Mayor, later Sir David Wootton, paid a visit to the Honourable Company for their annual dinner. A reciprocal arrangement exists between this organisation and the Guild of Freemen of the City of London, permitting attendance at each other's events.

In 1980 the Lord Mayor granted the Company permission to use the Coat of Arms of the City of London.

Another interesting link between the City of London and Canada is to be found in the small town of Mannville, Alberta. Mannville was the place of birth of Sir Peter Gadsden, Lord Mayor of London (1979-80) and the Founder Master of the Worshipful Company of Engineers. Despite moving to the UK at a very young age, Sir Peter retained his Canadian citizenship and worked to develop strong links between the UK and Canada. He is remembered in the town by an annual 'Lord Mayor of London Memorial Tea' held usually held on the last Friday in June.

Association of Liverymen in New Zealand

Efforts to form an association for Freemen and Liverymen in New Zealand have resulted in dinners at the Northern Club in Auckland during 2016 and 2017, the latter attended by the Master Air Pilot. The Lord Mayor of London visited the Association in Auckland in 2018. Plans for further events are at an advanced stage and they look set to become a regular fixture. The Association also collaborates with the Air Pilots' Company's New Zealand Region.

The Ancient Society of College Youths

This Society was founded in 1637 and is the world's leading society for the form of campanology known as 'change ringing'. The man who did so much to perfect this technique, Fabian Steadman, is buried at St Andrew Undershaft, and a plaque to his memory is in its entrance porch.

The Society is based in the City of London and promotes excellence in bell-ringing in the UK and internationally. Potential members must be at least 14 years old and have rung a quarter peal in a recognised method. The Society is headed by an annually elected Master and supported by a number of stewards. Curiously the Society excludes members of the Society of Royal Cumberland Youths, another leading society based in Westminster.

As is the wont of City institutions, the Ancient Society of College Youths counts among its youthful membership some who have recorded 50, 60 or even 70 years of service!

The Guild of Mercers 'Scholars

This organisation brings together former pupils of the various schools that the Mercers' Company supports. The Guild operates similarly to a Livery Company, electing its own Master from among a Court of Assistants. The Guild aims to help former pupils to develop an understanding of the City and its traditions, and maybe in time become members of a Livery Company relevant to their trade, craft, profession or interests.

The Guild of Scholars

This organisation, formed in 1998, brings together former students of the City of London schools, namely City of London School, City of London School for Girls, and City of London

Freemen's School. The Guild aims 'to raise the profile of the City within the schools' and vice versa through a series of annual events, outings and engagements with the City. The Guild has its own charitable trust that aims to provide bursaries and scholarships to those who might otherwise be unable to enter the City schools.

The Inner Temple and Middle Temple

The Inner Temple and Middle Temple, today home to the eponymous Honourable Societies, form two of the four Inns of Court for England and Wales. They are anomalies within a City full of anomalies in that they are separate local authorities inside the City limits. The Lord Mayor's writ does not run to the Inner Temple and Middle Temple, although by agreement they permit the City Police to operate on their premises and are subject to the authority of the Court of Common Council in respect of town planning and listed buildings.

Together with Lincoln's Inn and Gray's Inn, the Inner Temple and Middle Temple form the Inns of Court and have the exclusive right to call barristers to the bar. All barristers in England and Wales must belong to one of the four Inns. The Inner Temple and Middle Temple date from at least 1388. The Inns are structured in a similar manner to Oxford or Cambridge colleges and provide dinners, training and accommodation for their members.

The Inns have long had an association with the army, and many members serve in the Inns of Court and City Yeomanry, which is based in Lincoln's Inn (see The City and the Armed Forces).

The Bridge House Estates

This is probably one of the oldest charitable trusts in the City, founded in 1282 with the sole purpose of providing funds to maintain London Bridge. The income from rental properties and investments controlled by the Bridge House Estates far exceeds the needs of maintaining the five bridges that the City now administers, and since 1995 the City Bridge Foundation (previously the City Bridge Trust) has been able to disperse its surplus to a wide range of worthy charitable causes.

Properties owned by the Bridge House Estates are marked with a unique 'Bridge Mark'. Perhaps chief among the properties owned by the Bridge House Estates is the Central Criminal Court or Old Bailey.

The following bridges are those that the City maintains:

London Bridge - 1282
Blackfriars Bridge - 1769
Southwark Bridge - 1864

Tower Bridge - 1894
Millennium Bridge - 2000
(footbridge)

The City Heritage Society

In 1973 the City established a Conservation Area Advisory Committee [CAAC] and Common Councilman Douglas Woodward proposed that there should be a residents' representative on that committee.

This was accepted and the Barbican Residents' Association formed a subcommittee named the Barbican Association Conservation Group who then sent a member to sit on the CAAC. However, many non-Barbican residents concerned about conservation issues joined so in 1975 the name was changed to the City Heritage Society.

It continues to send a representative to sit on the CAAC and tries to monitor and all applications for planning consent in the City not just those in conservation areas. It was registered with the Civic Trust as the amenity society for the City and has charitable status.

In 1978 the City Heritage Award was instituted jointly with the Worshipful Company of Painter-Stainers. The Award is given annually to a project judged by a panel of assessors to be the best refurbishment/conservation project completed in the City of London in the previous year. It comprises a hand-crafted certificate awarded to the principal designer and a bronze plaque which are presented at a ceremony by the Lord Mayor.

In 1994 the Mansion House received the award after a significant overhaul conducted by the contractor Holloway White Allom.

A full list of the City Heritage Society award winners may be found in the appendices.

The Commission of Lieutenancy

Every year at Christmas the Monarch issues a new Commission of Lieutenancy for the City of London. The Commission exists to perform the role of the Lord Lieutenant as is appointed by the Monarch for other ceremonial counties. The first Commission of Lieutenancy was issued by King James I in 1617 and comprised the Lord Mayor, eight Aldermen and the Recorder of London.

There is no Lord Lieutenant, Vice Lord Lieutenant or Deputy Lieutenants for the City of London; members of the Commission of Lieutenancy are styled Lieutenants.

The Lord Mayor is Chairman of the Commission of Lieutenancy and outgoing Lord Mayor's have the right to nominate someone for appointment to the Commission for life. The Monarch makes the appointment at the same time as the new Commission of Lieutenancy is issued for the year ensuing.

All Late Lord Mayors are also members of the Commission. There are several members of the Commission who hold their office Ex Officio, including the Governor of the Bank of England, the Commissioner of the City of London Police, the Recorder of

London, the Common Sergeant and the Chairman of the City of London Reserve Forces and Cadets Association.

The Commission of Lieutenancy is the sole body with the authority to raise the Trophy Tax which it may spend for the upkeep of the armed forces of the Crown. That said it won't stretch very far as the tax was fixed at £4666 in 1820 and hasn't increased since! The Tax is levied on the Corporation of London by means of a Royal Warrant. In truth the Corporation also contributes considerably to the running of the City of London Reserve Forces and Cadets Association

The Lieutenants have the right and privilege to be received in person when presentating an address to the Monarch. This right was contested early in the 20th century but was upheld during the short reign of King Edward VIII.

While the number of Lieutenant varies owing to the lifetime appointment of the Lord Mayor's nominee, the Militia Act (1882) sets the minimum size of the Commission at 20 persons.

The Badge of the Commission of Lieutenancy, a unique example of the City of London's Arms surmounted by a symbol of Royal authority.

Private Members' Clubs

Few private members' clubs exist in the City, partly because of the small size of the resident population, and because the Livery Companies, Guilds, and Societies provide for an ample social scene. The City Livery Club has already been mentioned. The other notable clubs in the City are:

The City of London Club

This club was founded in 1832 and is on Old Broad Street. The club is limited to 1,400 members and extended full membership to ladies only in 2011. Founding members of the club include the first Duke of Wellington and Sir Robert Peel.

The City University Club

This club was founded in 1895 and was, until the spring of 2018, located on Cornhill. It has now merged premises with the Lloyds Club (below). Its membership was originally restricted to graduates of Oxford and Cambridge universities, but is now open to all.

The Lloyds Club

The Lloyds Club was founded in 1920. It has occupied various premises in the City and is now at the rather unusual address of 42 Crutched Friars.

The Little Ship Club

Founded in 1926, it is the only sailing club with a City home. The clubhouse is adjacent to Southwark Bridge and shares its premises with the City Livery Club.

The London Capital Club / Gresham Club

The London Capital Club was founded in 1994, located on Abchurch Lane. It closed its doors in the summer of 2018. This was of the more recent clubs to open in the City, although it has strong historical links to the now defunct Gresham Club originally founded in 1843 and occupying the same site. The London Capital Club is where the Guild of Entrepreneurs was founded in 2014.

Since closing its doors a group of former members of the London Capital Club have sought to re-establish the Gresham Club, albeit in a new location yet to be determined. At the time of writing the club has put itself on a solid foot for growth and seeks to open premises in the City.

The Walbrook Club

This little City gem of a club opened its doors in 2000. The club resides in a Queen Anne-style building behind Mansion House. It is a weekday dining club with a bar and meeting facilities.

The Eight Club

Opened in 2006 this club is unique in occupying two locations: 1 Dysart Street (EC2) and 1 Change Alley (EC3). The club is also unique in offering a virtual London office and landline package for members in addition to dining facilities and a fitness gym at the Dysart Street location.

Brand Exchange

Located on Birchin Lane in a grade II listed building, the Brand Exchange opened in 2015. It is a meeting venue and members' club aimed at City professionals with an interest in finance and brands.

Searcys Club at the Gherkin

This club is at the apex of the Gherkin (30 St Mary Axe) and is connected with the restaurant of the same name. The restaurant is normally open to members and business tenants but is also available for public bookings on selected dates during the year.

Guildhall Club

The Guildhall Club is a restricted membership club for elected officers of the City of London, including the Lord Mayor, Aldermen, Sheriffs and Common Councilmen. Membership is also open to past elected officers who served a minimum of 6 years.

Ten Trinity Square (Four Seasons Hotel)

Opened in the winter of 2017 and describing itself as the City's finest private club for business, wine and culture, Ten Trinity Square is also the only club with a cigar lounge.

Ned's Club (Ned Hotel)

This club is part of the Ned Hotel and features a rooftop heated pool, outdoor terrace, gym, spa and underground 'vault' bar that offers live entertainment.

The City's Royal Connections

If posterity shall ask who would have pulled down the Crown from the King's head, taken the government off its hinges, dissolved monarchy, enslaved the laws, and ruined their country; say 'twas the proud, unthankful, schismatic, rebellious, bloody, City of London.

From a royalist pamphlet printed during the English Civil War.

HRH The Earl of Wessex with Charles Hughes, then Master of the Worshipful Company of Information Technologists at Mansion House at the presentation of the Company's Royal Charter in June 2010. Photograph courtesy of Jonathan Histed.

About the City's once uneasy relationship with the Crown much has been said and written. Such comments are often ill-informed and recycle opinions from many centuries past. The City's relationship with the Crown has improved beyond recognition from the dark days of the Civil War when Charles I left London to set up court in Oxford owing to the rebellious and threatening nature of the City of London.

The City's partnership with the Crown had transformed so greatly in the 360 years since the Civil War that on 30th June 1943 Prime Minister Winston Churchill spoke the following words at Guildhall on being admitted as a Freeman of the City of London:

> *'Of all our institutions there is none which has served us better in the hour of need than our ancient monarchy around which all that we have is centred.'*

The City's connections with royalty go back at least as far as Edward the Confessor. The City was an important source of tax revenues and loans for successive monarchs, and in return the City acquired increasing powers and political independence through a series of Royal Charters, the earliest extant of which is the one sealed by William the Conqueror and on display at Guildhall.

Past monarchs have been members of Livery Companies, including Queen Elizabeth I who was a Free Sister of the Mercers' Company. Another Queen Elizabeth, HM Queen Elizabeth The Queen Mother, was a Freeman of the Butchers' Company and the Grocers' Company.

No Livery Company banquet is complete without the Loyal Toast, usually followed by a toast in honour of the other members of the Royal Family.

His Majesty King Charles III is Permanent Master of the Shipwrights, Royal Patron of the Air Pilots, Past Master of the Master Mariners, Court Assistant of the Goldsmiths, Royal Liveryman of the Gardeners, Honorary Liveryman of the Carpenters, Brewers, Farmers, Fruiterers, Stationers, Pewterers; Freeman of the Drapers and Fishmongers, and Honorary Freeman of the Musicians. His Majesty is also Captain General of the Honourable Artillery Company.

HM Queen Camilla being clothed with the livery of the Fan Makers' Company in February 2024. Both the Master (behind Her Majesty) and the Free Warden (to Her Majesty's right) were colleagues of the author during his military service. Photograph kindly provided by the Fan Makers' Company.

Her Majesty Queen Camilla is an Honorary Liveryman of the Plaisterers, the Joiners and Ceilers, the Plumbers, the Vintners, and most recently the Fan Makers in 2024.

It is believed that Her Majesty's clothing was the first such clothing of a Queen consort during her husband's reign.

Many senior members of the Royal Family are also members of Livery Companies; some have served as Master or Prime Warden of one or more Companies. The following incomplete list illustrates some of the Royal Family's connections with several of the Livery Companies:

- HRH The Prince of Wales – Liveryman of the Air Pilots

- HRH The Duke of York – Grand Master of the Air Pilots, Liveryman of the Shipwrights

- HRH The Princess Royal – Past Master of the Butchers, Carmen, Farmers, Farriers, Loriners, Woolmen, Master Mariners and Guild of Freemen; Past Prime Warden of the Fishmongers, Perpetual Master of The Saddlers, Liveryman of the Engineers

- HRH The Duke of Edinburgh – Royal Master of the Fuellers, Past Master of the Gardeners, Court Assistant of the Haberdashers, Honorary Liveryman of the Coopers

- HRH The Duke of Gloucester - Patron of the Pattenmakers, Liveryman of the Masons, Honorary Liveryman of the Basketmakers, Vintners and of the Goldsmiths; Honorary Freeman of the Grocers.

- HRH The Duchess of Gloucester – Liveryman of the Fan Makers, Honorary Liveryman of the Gold and Silver Wyre Drawers, Liveryman of the Vintners, Honorary Liveryman of the Basketmakers, Honorary Freeman of the Drapers

- HRH The Duke of Kent – Liveryman of the Salters, Liveryman of the Mercers, Honorary Liveryman of the Clothworkers, Honorary Liveryman and Assistant Emeritus of the Engineers, Honorary Freeman of the Musicians and of the Apothecaries

- HRH The Duchess of Kent - Freeman of the Coachmakers & Coach Harness Makers, Freeman of the Dyers, Honorary Freeman of the Musicians, Honorary Freeman of the Glaziers and Painters of Glass and of the Clothworkers

- HRH Prince Michael of Kent - Liveryman the Air Pilots, Clothworkers, Coachmakers and Coach Harness Makers, Leathersellers, and Scientific Instrument Makers

- HRH Princess Michael of Kent - Honorary Freeman of the Gardeners, Weavers and Goldsmiths

- HRH Princess Alexandra – Royal Honorary Freeman of the Barbers, Honorary Freeman of the Clothworkers

Queen Elizabeth II was a Freeman of the City of London, Patron of the Shipwrights' Company, the Master Mariners' Company and the Air Pilots' Company, a Draper by Patrimony and Captain General of the Honourable Artillery Company (HAC). Queen Elizabeth II took an active interest in the life of the HAC, having last presented colours to the Regiment in May 2007.

On 31st May 2017 Queen Elizabeth II visited the Drapers' Hall to celebrate 70 years as a Freeman of the Company. During the visit she was elected to the Court. The Master called a vote on the matter and asked if there were any members who wished to vote to the contrary. A less than commodious apartment at HM Tower of London remained vacant for another evening and Queen Elizabeth II was elected unanimously.

Perhaps the most prolific Liveryman among the Royal Family was HRH The Prince Philip, Duke of Edinburgh. Among his many City affiliations were the following:

Patron and Past Grand Master of the Air Pilots, Admiral of the Master Mariners, Past Prime Warden of the Fishmongers, Permanent Master of the Shipwrights, First Liveryman of the Engineers, Liveryman of the Mercers, Freeman of the Coachmakers & Coach Harness Makers and of the Ironmongers, Honorary Freeman of the Environmental Cleaners and of the Marketors, Honorary Freeman of the Musicians. He was also Patron of the City of London Club, Honorary Member of the City Livery Club, Royal Bencher of the Inner Temple and a member of the Honourable Artillery Company.

Note: No offence is meant to any member of the Royal Family or to any Livery Company whose links are not listed above.

It seems certain that younger members of the Royal Family will take their place among the ranks of the Livery in due course.

Royal Portraits

The City Livery Companies have a long tradition of commissioning royal portraits. Companies such as the Drapers and Fishmongers have particularly notable portraits of national significance. The famous Annigoni portrait of Queen Elizabeth II, which hangs in Fishmongers' Hall, was commissioned by that Company at the suggestion of her late husband HRH The Duke of Edinburgh.

Queen Elizabeth II with the Master Draper (seated), Wardens, Clerk and Beadle of the Company on the occasion of her elevation to the Court in May 2017. With kind permission of the Drapers' Company.

Portrait of Queen Elizabeth II commissioned by the Drapers' Company and painted by Sergei Pavlenko. The painting is believed to be the late Queen's favourite since her coronation. It was unveiled in 2000 and hangs in Drapers' Hall. With kind permission of the Drapers' Company.

On the occasion of the Queen Elizabeth II's Diamond Jubilee, the Livery Companies of the City of London entertained Her Majesty to lunch at Westminster Hall. The then Master Mercer gave a speech on behalf of the Livery that evidences the very close relationship between the Livery and the Crown today. A transcript of that speech is on the Mercers' Company website.

Presentations from several Livery Companies are made to members of the Royal Family on special occasions, including gloves from the Glovers' Company and flowers from the Gardeners' Company. The Girdlers' Company provides the sword belt and stole that the Sovereign wears during a coronation. The Saddlers' Company has on long-term loan the saddle used by the King's (or Queen's) Champion - an office held by the Lord of the Manor of Scrivelsby in Lincolnshire.

As Royal Charter Corporations, the Livery Companies also have the right to petition the Monarch, via the Privy Council, on matters pertaining to their charters such as infringement of their rights and privileges by another body. Through the granting of a Royal Charter, a Company can also represent their trade, craft or profession to Parliament.

Buckingham Palace Garden Parties

For many years it has been the custom for Livery Company Masters and their spouse or consort to be invited to one of the garden parties held in the grounds of Buckingham Palace each year. The Lord Mayor, Sheriffs and Aldermen also receive an annual invitation to the garden parties.

Coronation Banquet

Should there ever be another coronation banquet, the Lord Mayor of London has the right to assist the Chief Butler of England in serving the Monarch and by custom receives as his fee the golden cup from which the Monarch drinks during the banquet. However, no coronation banquet has occurred since that of George IV when the Lord Mayor assisted by 12 other principal officers of the City last had the honour to perform this duty. A coronation banquet was planned in 1902 for Edward VII but his illness before the coronation caused the banquet to be cancelled. That said a Coronation Cup was presented to Queen

Elizabeth II, gift of the Goldsmiths' Company, and was later returned to the Company's safe keeping.

The King's Bargemaster and Royal Watermen

The Port of London Authority owns and maintains a motor launch, the Royal Nore, for the Royal Family to use when on official business on the river Thames. The King's 24 Royal Watermen, including several past winners of the Doggett's Coat and Badge race, are chosen from among the Freemen of the Watermen and Lightermen's Company and are led by The King's Bargemaster. It is considered a great honour to be appointed a Royal Waterman, each of whom receives a handsome scarlet uniform and an annual salary of £18.00.

On the occasion of the Queen Elizabeth II's Diamond Jubilee, the lead vessel in the river pageant was Gloriana, the newly commissioned Royal Barge. QRB Gloriana is based on the design of barges used by past Lord Mayors and is used by the Lord Mayor during the annual River Progress.

Coronations

The Lord Mayor is the only elected government official who participates in the coronation ceremony. The Lord Mayor's place is on the dais with the monarch, clergy and high officers of state. During the coronation the Lord Mayor wears a unique Coronation Robe (see Uniforms of the Principal City Officers) and carries the City's Crystal Sceptre, a gift from Henry V to the City of London for its support during his campaigns in France. The Sceptre was first displayed in public on 2015 some 600 years after its presentation to the City.

Despite its diminutive size (17 inches) the Crystal Sceptre has been described as the greatest "thank you" gift in English history. The sceptre is on show during the Silent Ceremony and coronations.

The anniversary of the Coronation, royal birthdays and the state opening or prorogation of parliament are all celebrated with a gun salute from the Tower of London. The HAC fires 62 rounds from the Tower of London; 21 for the Sovereign; 20 for the Tower as a Royal Palace; and a further 21 for the City of London.

The Lord Mayor, Aldermen and Sheriffs are, by custom, invited to witness the Accession Council in St James's Palace, and attend the Proclamation delivered by one of the Kings of Arms on the steps of the Royal Exchange.

The Livery's involvement in the Coronation was evident in the richly embroidered screen that surrounded King Charles III during his anointing. It was a gift from the City of London and many of the Livery Companies.

Loyal Addresses

The City of London Corporation is one of 27 Privileged Bodies who are permitted to present a Loyal Address (previously known as a Humble Address) to the Monarch at significant events such as Accessions, Coronation and Jubilees. The Loyal Address is an opportunity for the City to reaffirm its important status, and in time past it also afforded an occasion to raise issues directly with the Monarch. The Loyal Address is always delivered by a senior member of the body concerned, which in the case of the Corporation would normally be the Lord Mayor.

Other City institutions that feature among those 27 Privileged Bodies are: The City of London Commission of Lieutenancy (Headed by the Lord Mayor); The Dean and Chapter of St Paul's Cathedral, and The Bank of England.

Ranger of Epping Forest

In 1878 the Epping Forest Act disafforested part of the ancient Royal Forest of Waltham, now forming Epping Forest and transferred ownership to the Lord Mayor, Aldermen and Commonality of the City of London.

The act makes provision for the Crown to appoint a Ranger with powers and duties as defined in his or her royal warrant. The Ranger must approve any by-laws introduced for the governance of the forest by the Court of Common Council's Epping Forest

Committee who are Conservators of the forest. The present Ranger of Epping Force is HRH The Duke of Gloucester.

By virtue of the Epping Forest Act (1878) the Conservators also became owners of Queen Elizabeth I's Hunting Lodge which is located adjacent to the Epping Forest Visitor Centre on Ranger's Road in the forest, surely the only example of a local authority owning and managing a former royal hunting lodge. The City of London Corporation also owns the adjacent Royal Forest Hotel, which was named by Queen Victoria in 1882. The arms of the City of London may be seen in stained glass in the hotel.

Epping Forest has one of three surviving Verderers' Courts in England, dating from the early 13th century these courts governed Forest Law in the Royal Hunting Forests. The other Verderers' Courts in England are for the Royal Forest of Dean and the New Forest.

The Verderers (Keepers of Epping Forest) are elected every 7 years from among the commoners living in the Forest, two for the northern parishes in the forest, two for the southern parishes. Verderers may not be members of the Court of Common Council. Together with 12 elected members of the Court of Common Council the Verderers form the Epping Forest Committee.

Heraldry and the Livery Companies

The Livery Companies have a unique and long-standing relationship with the art and science of heraldry, not least because they were the first corporate bodies to be formally granted arms. Prior to the Drapers' Company being granted its coat of arms in 1439, all grants by the Crown had been to people rather than to corporate entities. Examples exist of earlier use of heraldry by corporate entities, such as the City of London's own arms devised in or before 1381. The City's arms have never formally been granted but are recorded at HM College of Arms on Queen Victoria Street.

The arms, crest and supporters of the Information Technologists' Company displayed on a flag flying from IT Hall in the City.

The Livery Companies use their corporate arms extensively on robes, insignia, treasures, merchandise, stationery, website and even on social media. A Livery Company usually approaches HM College of Arms to *petition* (apply) for a Grant of Arms when it reaches the status of a City Company without Livery. A Company usually wishes to obtain arms before its elevation to full Livery Company status so that it may use the arms as a form of insignia.

Livery Companies are deemed to be sufficiently eminent corporate bodies to warrant supporters to their arms (i.e., animals, human figures or real or mythical beasts on either side of the shield), a distinction otherwise reserved for royalty, peers and knights of certain orders. Curiously the Mercers, despite being first in order of precedence, do not have supporters for their arms, and neither do the following Companies: Brewers, Carpenters, Cordwainers, Environmental Cleaners, Founders, Furniture Makers, Girdlers, Gunmakers, Horners, Musicians, Pattenmakers, Solicitors, Tylers and Bricklayers, or Woolmen.

Arms of the Grocers' Company on display in that Company's hall. The supporters either side of the shield are sign of the high status of the Company.

A recent grant of supporters to existing arms was to the Fan Makers in 2016: a pair of griffins. The initial design based upon putti (scantily clad male cherubs) waving fans was reported by the Heraldry Gazette as *'not being what the Master and Wardens had in mind'*.

Some of the most ancient of the Livery Companies have long used arms by assumption (without a legal grant), although all but one has been retrospectively registered with HM College of Arms. As an example, the Mercers' Company arms were formally recorded at the College of Arms as recently as 1911. Only the Loriners' Company has get to put its arms on a regular footing.

Several Livery Companies proudly display the coats of arms of Past Masters in their Livery Hall. Noteworthy examples include the Armourers & Brasiers, Founders, Ironmongers and Stationers.

Eligibility for a Grant of Arms is not limited to Masters, Prime Wardens or Upper Bailiffs. Liverymen who aspire to armorial bearings i.e., a shield of arms, badge, crest (male only) and standard are advised not to wait until they might be elected Master. Ladies and gentlemen who are subjects of the Crown, of good moral character, who can provide evidence of their eminence and have the financial means to petition are usually eligible. This definition will happily import most of the Livery. A letter or email to the Officer in Waiting at HM College of Arms starts the process, or if you happen to know one of the Heralds or Pursuivants and prefer to work with them, you may contact that officer directly. Liverymen who are normally resident in Scotland may prefer to contact the Court of Lord Lyon in Edinburgh.

HM College of Arms also maintains the official register of family pedigrees and can research and record family genealogy. Liverymen may have their status (as a Liveryman), academic and professional qualifications, crown honours and commonwealth military decorations recorded in the pedigree. Originals of full birth, marriage and death certificates and any adoptions or divorces expedites the College's research

Among the senior elected officers of the City, the Aldermen are expected to obtain a Grant of Arms if they do not already have their own arms by inheritance. Sheriffs are required to obtain arms in time for the presentation of their Royal Warrant at the ceremony of the Quit Rents. The Lord Mayor must have arms and will have obtained them earlier in the progression to the chair, either as Alderman or Sheriff, if not inherited.

Note: Heraldic convention, sometimes called 'heraldic law' does not currently treat men and women as equals. Women are not entitled to a crest, should display their marital status on their arms (single, married, divorced, widowed) and their children may not inherit arms granted to a woman unless she seeks and obtains a Royal Licence.

The Lord Mayor, Sheriffs and Aldermen also have heraldic banners which are paraded in the Lord Mayor's Show, usually carried by a cadet from one of the cadet forces following the Lord Mayor's coach. The heraldic banners of the present and former Lord Mayors who are still Aldermen are displayed in the Aldermen's Court at Guildhall.

The heraldry of the Livery Companies has spread beyond the City of London. No shortage of public houses in England take as their name the arms of a Livery Company. Many of the provincial Guilds also use arms that are similar or identical to those of the City of London Livery Companies - a bold and blatant transgression of the law of arms that has perhaps not yet reached the attention of the Earl Marshal's Court.

A fantastic source of further learning about heraldry and coats of arms is the Heraldry Society, the learned society for the study of the subject. The Scriveners' Company sponsors an annual lecture by the Heraldry Society and that Company's Master along with the Masters of the Glaziers' Company and the Painter-Stainers' Company are ex-officio Honorary Vice Presidents of the Heraldry Society.

Another organisation with its origins in the City is the White Lion Society, founded in 1986 to support the work of the College of Arms. Membership is open to all.

Arms of Past Masters of the Armourers' & Brasiers' Company on display in Armourers' Hall.

Uniforms of the Principal City Officers

The Lord Mayor

The Lord Mayor has no fewer than five ceremonial outfits for different occasions. The scarlet robe of an Alderman with black velvet and edged with sable fur is the most widely recognised and is usually worn with the Lord Mayor's iconic tricorn hat.

The Lord Mayor and Aldermen also have violet robes that are worn for most City meetings. This robe is similar to the scarlet robe and is edged with black Canadian bear fur in place of sable.

For City banquets and some of the services held at St Paul's, the Lord Mayor wears the Black Robe of State. This is made of black silk damask and, like the hem and collar, is trimmed with two and a quarter inches of gold lace. The sleeves, sides and train of this robe have gold wire ornaments.

On occasions when the Lord Mayor receives the Sovereign, the Crimson Velvet Robe of State appears. This follows the same design as an earl's coronation robe and is furred with miniver.

The least frequently worn robe is the magnificent Coronation Robe. It is made of crimson velvet lined with white silk satin and adorned with four bars of miniver powdered with black fur below wide gold lace which extends across both fronts back to the side seams. The edging, collar and train also have gold lace ornamentation. The shoulders are decorated with large cream silk rosettes. This robe is unique and is only worn during the Coronation ceremony when the Lord Mayor carries the crystal sceptre. The last time the robe was worn was in 1953 for the Coronation of Queen Elizabeth the Second. The Lord Mayor at the time was Alderman Sir Rupert de la Bere, Citizen & Skinner. His Coronation robe is kept in Skinners' Hall and is still used in the Company's annual childrens' Christmas party

The Sheriffs

For civic ceremonial occasions, the City's two Sheriffs wear Aldermanic robes of either scarlet or violet depending on the occasion. The uniform is the same regardless of whether the Sheriff is an Alderman.

The Sheriffs wear court dress to dinners at Mansion House and other important functions. The code for court dress was laid down in 1869 by the Lord Chamberlain and comprises a coat and breeches of black silk velvet with cut steel buttons, shoes with cut steel buckles, a white lace jabot (neck piece) with matching shirt cuffs, black leggings and a sword.

The Aldermen

The scarlet robe forms the basis of ceremonial dress for Aldermen and is identical to that worn by the Lord Mayor except that the current and past holders of the latter office have what is sometimes called a cap of honour attached to the back of the robe just below their right shoulder, however this is actually a vestige of a hood. Aldermen occasionally wear a bicorn hat, especially when parading in the Lord Mayor's Show.

The Livery Company Masters, Wardens and Clerks

Each Livery Company has its own robes and insignia for the senior officers of the Court and they differ in precise detail of their design and colours from one Company to the next. Generally the colours used in the robes of Livery Company officers are taken from the first two colours in the Company's coat of arms, although this does not guarantee unique colour combinations.

The shape of the Master's robe is usually similar to an Oxford or Cambridge MA gown with a 'boot' sleeve slit just above the elbow. Many of the older Companies trim their Master's robe with fur, although the trend is towards synthetic alternatives for reasons of cost and ethics. The Master's gown might also feature a hood or the vestiges of one permanently sewn onto the rear of the robe. Most of the younger Companies have the Company's coat of arms embroidered on the sleeve of the Master's robe.

The Wardens' robe is usually based on the Master's one with a conventional sleeve and less ornamentation.

The Clerk's robe is usually plain black and follows a design similar to that of a King's Counsel. The Clerk's robe may be augmented with rows of tuffs (or tassels) on the sleeves and body of the gown and usually includes Cambridge doctoral lace on the sleeves.

Gauntlets and gloves worn by the Master of the Glovers' Company. The gauntlets are richly embroidered with the arms of the Company.

The Master's Robe of the Pattenmakers' Company with detail of the Company's arms. Photo courtesy of Kenneth Crawford (www.robesofdistinction.org.uk).

The City and the Armed Forces

As with so many other aspects of the City, its relationship with the Armed Forces of the Crown is unique. Whereas in all other parts of the Sovereign's realm, members of HM Armed Forces may proceed freely under their commander's orders, in the City of London, no troops may enter without the prior permission of the Lord Mayor. This common law right of the City was tested and upheld in court in 1842. The right stems from a charter granted to the Mayor and Commonality of the City of London by King Edward III in 1327.

The Livery Companies have long supported the Armed Forces and most Companies continue to support one or more units of the regular, reserve or cadet forces. The liveries' support to affiliated Armed Forces unit will usually encompass prize giving; awards; publicity; sporting and social events; career enrichment and mentorship of service personnel at key stages in their career.

Some Companies have an obvious connection based on common professional interest and shared membership, such as the Information Technologists and the Royal Signals (the Army's IT and communications combat support arm), or the Engineers' Company, which makes awards for excellence in engineering to the Royal Navy, Army and Royal Air Force.

The City Livery profile produced by the Mercers' Company in 2011 identified no fewer than 216 regular or reserve Armed Forces units supported by Livery Companies. A list of most, though not all, Livery Company affiliations with the Armed Forces is on the website of the Greater London Reserve Forces and Cadets Association (see Online Resources).

In times past, various ancient Livery Companies were required to fund or raise troops for the trained bands of London. The trained bands were volunteer companies whose officers were members of the Honourable Artillery Company, itself structured similarly to a Livery Company. In modern times the HAC's Company of

Pikemen and Musketeers has received material support including new muskets, gloves and mittens from City Livery Companies.

Many serving and retired members of HM Armed Forces are members of one or more Livery Companies. Many Companies employ retired officers as their Clerk and retired senior non-commissioned officers or warrant officers as their Beadle.

The Lord Mayor also supports the Armed Forces in various ways, including the appointment from among the Cadet Forces leadership of several military Aides-de-Camp, all of whom are volunteer officers. The ADCs, who are appointed for a minimum of two years, play a role in supporting the Lord Mayor to facilitate wider and deeper links between the City, its Livery Companies and the various Cadet Forces. The ADCs wear a distinctive silver aiguillette over the left shoulder of their uniform and may be seen on parade at events such as the Lord Mayor's Show.

The Lord Mayor further supports the Armed Forces through the annual Big Curry Lunch at Guildhall. This event is held in partnership with and in support of ABF The Soldiers' Charity (the Army Benevolent Fund).

In 2013 the Garrison Sergeant Major London District, WO1 (GSM) William Mott OBE MVO was admitted as a Freeman of the City of London in recognition of his many years' service to the Crown and the City, especially in respect of his role in state ceremonial occasions.

The following military units have been granted the privilege of marching in the City with colours flying, drums beating and bayonets fixed (ie. City privileged 'regiment' status):

- HMS Westminster (since 2005)
- HMS President (since 2016)
- The Royal Marines (since at least 1924)[†]
- The Blues and Royals (from the Royal Dragoons) (1961)[†]

- The Grenadier Guards (since at least 1904)[†]
- The Coldstream Guards (since 1952)
- The Princess of Wales's Royal Regiment (from the Royal East Kent Regiment) (since at least 1746)[†]
- The London Regiment (since 1995)
- The Royal Regiment of Fusiliers (since 1924)
- 101 (City of London) Engineer Regiment (EOD) (2015) - the author's former regiment
- The Honourable Artillery Company (since 1924)[†]
- 3 Military Intelligence Battalion (since 2017)
- 600 (City of London) Squadron Royal Auxiliary Air Force (since 2007)
- First Aid Nursing Yeomanry (Princess Royal's Volunteer Corps) (since 2021)

[†] These units, or their antecedents, have exercised their right by ancient custom long before it was formally granted. These privileged regiments of the City of London are sometimes erroneously described as having 'the Freedom of the City'. The Freedom of the City of London is granted only to individuals and not to organisations including military units.

When exercising their right, these privileged units are met by the City Marshal, who challenges them as follows:

Who comes there?

The Commanding Officer of the military detachment then replies (for example):

The First Battalion Coldstream Guards exercising their ancient privilege and right to enter the City of London with colours flying, drums beating and bayonets fixed.

The City Marshal responds (for example):

I have it on the authority of the Lord Mayor to receive and attend your Battalion through the City.

The City Marshal then salutes and leads the troops into the City.

Other regiments associated with the City of London include:

- The Inns of Court & City Yeomanry, which is part of 71 (City of London) Yeomanry Signal Regiment
- 39 (Skinners) Signals Regiment, which is the only regiment with a named Livery Company in its title
- 256 (City of London) Field Hospital, which has three detachments (A,B, and C) affiliated with the Apothecaries, Barbers, and Cutlers
- The Rifles, which provide an honour guard at the Lord Mayor's Banquet on the Monday following the Lord Mayor's Show and have a plaque in Guildhall with those of other regiments affiliated with the City.

Note: The inclusion of 'City of London' (usually in brackets) in a regiment or squadron title does not imply City privileged status but rather that the unit has a special relationship with the City of London that is recognised by the Court of Aldermen and conferred by the Lord Mayor.

Possibly one of the least known of the annual City ceremonies is the presentation, by the Lord Mayor, of the Cutlers' Company Sword to the non-commissioned officer judged to have the highest potential from among the Corps of Drums and Bugles of the five regiments of Foot Guards (Grenadier, Coldstream, Scots, Irish and Welsh) and the English and Welsh line regiments. The sword is presented outside Mansion House during the Lord Mayor's Show just before the Lord Mayor joins the parade in the State Coach.

The City, Livery and Philanthropy

The Livery Companies collectively donate tens of millions of pounds to charitable causes each year. The Livery Profile commissioned by the Mercers' Company provides a high-level analysis of the charitable disbursements of the Livery as a whole, as does the report by the Pan Livery Initiative in 2018. While it is impossible to be precise about the total value of philanthropic activity undertaken by the Livery it is almost certainly more than £80m when financial disbursements and funding in kind is considered.

What can never be measured with any accuracy is the value of time and talent donated by Freemen and Liverymen to good causes, whether as school governors, charity trustees, mentors to journeymen and school pupils, or donating their professional expertise *pro bono*. The moral support afforded to various organisations, not least the armed forces, should also be considered an example of this philanthropic activity.

It would be invidious to list individual Livery Company philanthropic endeavours; they are too numerous and wide-ranging to be adequately covered in this concise guide. That said, various City-wide initiatives are worth a mention:

The Lord Mayor's Appeal

During the mayoral year, the Lord Mayor selects a theme and various charitable beneficiaries. They receive support from the Lord Mayor's Appeal, which in turn raises funds from many social and sporting events during the year. In recent years, the Lord Mayor's Appeal has been restructured to provide a more sustained period of support to charitable causes, with some causes supported for a three-year period.

A Better City for All

An example of the multi-year approach to philanthropy in the City is the strategy titled 'A Better City for All', which encompasses: an inclusivity and diversity programme, a workplace mental health programme, a skills programme with particular emphasis on young women, and a fairness programme in the guise of City Giving Day.

City Giving Day

First launched in 1990, City Giving Day is an opportunity for businesses and individuals to focus on community support, volunteering, corporate social responsibility and charitable giving. In 2015, some 205 businesses in the City took part and over 3,000 new volunteers signed up to support community and charity projects.

The Dragon Awards

Founded in 1987, the Lord Mayor's Dragon Awards recognise excellence in corporate social responsibility across the whole of London in various categories spanning learning, employment and community partnership.

The City Bridge Foundation

The proceeds of the City Bridge Founsation's various estates are substantially greater than is required to maintain the City's five bridges, and since 1995 the City Bridge Foundation has been able to support a wide range of charities and good causes. The Foundation is governed by elected members of the Court of Common Council.

The Sheriffs '& Recorder's Fund

Set up in 1808 to help the inmates of Newgate Prison, the Sheriffs' & Recorder's Fund exists to help London's former prisoners and their families. The fund gives small grants to improve the lives of ex-offenders by providing training, trade tools, clothing, furniture and equipment, and support for families of former convicts. The overall aim is to reduce recidivism and works mainly through the probation service.

Livery Climate Action Group (LiveryCAG)

This group of Livery Companies, Companies without Livery and Guilds was formed in 2021 and collaborates to help the City of London meet the objectives of its climate strategy to achieve net zero by 2040, specifically by reducing carbon emissions and making responsible use of resources.

Pollinating London Together (PLT)

PLT is a joint initiative by the City of London Corporation and a network of Livery Companies was launched in 2020 to create spaces in central London where all the natural pollinators can thrive, and their habitats can be enjoyed with everyone, starting in the City of London. PLI has since grown to embrace non-Livery members including Historic Royal Palaces, Chelsea Physic Garden and other institutions

The City's Support for Education

The roots of early Guild and Livery Company involvement with education stem from their historical role in training apprentices. An apprentice would be indentured to a Master, typically for up to seven years. The apprentice had a duty to study hard, obey his Master and keep away from drink and gambling. In return the Master was responsible for providing board and lodging, training in a trade, craft or profession, and acting *in loco parentis*.

The Lord Mayor of London, Alderman Professor Michael Mainelli presenting a Master Coachmaker certificate accompanied by the Master of the Coachmakers and Coach Hardness Makers' Company. Photograph copyright the Coachmakers' Company.

The Livery Companies Skills Council (LCSC)

One way in which the Livery continues to support technical education is through the Livery Company Skills Council and its Master Certificate Scheme which is run in collaboration with City & Guilds of London (the examining and awarding body). The scheme supports progression beyond National Vocational Qualifications (NVQs) and operates at three levels: Apprentice, Journeyman and Master. At the time of writing 21 of the City's Livery Companies support the scheme and provide mentorship, training, professional development and practical assistance to craft skills practitioners.

Professional Recognition Award

In addition to the Master Certificate Scheme, the Livery Company Skills Council offers a Professional Recognition Award which is operated and issued by City & Guilds of London. The Award recognises personal commitment and demonstrates to employers the leadership and management skills needed alongside technical qualifications for candidates to progress successfully in their chosen careers. The Award is positioned at Level 4 in the National Qualifications Framework (NQF) and results in the post nominals LCGI (Licentiateship of City and Guilds of London Institute).

Apprenticeships within the Livery

Some Livery Companies still continue the tradition of apprenticeship, albeit adapted for modern times. One such example is the Goldsmiths' Company which still admits apprentices, many of whom go on to become craft jewellers, others work for the Assay Office on in allied roles.

Most Companies maintain links with education through such diverse activities as providing school governors, student awards, student bursaries, postgraduate and doctoral research grants, and charitable donations to educational institutions.

In 2014 the Livery Companies Apprenticeship Scheme enrolled its first batch of 52 apprentices both traditional and modern, to support the various small businesses allied to their particular trade, craft or profession.

City of London Corporation Schools

The City of London is unique among local government authorities in the UK in having responsibility for several private schools, in addition to sponsoring one sixth form, six academies and three primary schools. The schools are as follows:

- The Aldgate School (state-maintained, voluntary-aided Church of England school)
- The City Hackney Academy (co-sponsored with KPMG)
- The City of London Academy, Islington (co-sponsored with City University)
- The City of London Academy, Southwark (sponsored by the
- The City of London Academy, Highgate Hill
- The City of London Academy, Shoreditch Park
- The City of London Academy, Highbury Grove
- Newham Collegiate Sixth Form, City of London Academy
- City and supported by various Livery Companies and Ward Clubs)
- Redriff Primary City of London Academy in Southwark
- The City of London Primary Academy Islington
- Galleywall Primary School in Southwark
- The City of London School (Independent)
- The City of London Girls' School (Independent)
- City of London Freemen's School (Independent)
- The Guildhall School of Music and Drama (Independent)

Livery Company Schools

Livery Companies have built and founded many schools, and have links with more than 150 schools and colleges and many universities. In 2010 the Livery Companies donated over 20 million pounds to education (Livery Profile, 2011). The newest school founded by the Livery is Hammersmith Academy (2011), jointly funded by the Mercers' Company and the Information Technologists' Company.

Some notable schools associated with the City of London and the Livery Companies include:

- St Paul's School and St Paul's Girls' School in London (Mercers);
- Haberdashers' Aske's Boys' and Girls' Schools at Elstree and the Haberdashers' Aske's Federation Trust, a multi-academy trust of three academies in south-east London along with five schools elsewhere in England and Wales;
- Oundle School near Peterborough (Grocers);
- Colfe's School in Lewisham (Leathersellers);
- Tonbridge School (Skinners);
- Gresham's School in Norfolk (Fishmongers); and
- The City of London Freemen's School in Ashtead.

Christ's Hospital, the original and oldest Bluecoat School, in Horsham, has a special link with the City. The school was founded in 1552 by Edward VI in Newgate Street but relocated to Horsham in West Sussex in 1902. The school's band has the unique privilege of being able to march in the City of London, and appears in the Lord Mayor's Show and the annual St Matthew's Day parade that terminates in Guildhall Yard where the Lord Mayor takes the salute of the school before all the pupils march in to lunch.

Another school that has particularly strong links with the City and the Lord Mayor is Treloar's School in Alton. The school was opened in 1908 as a result of a public appeal by Sir William

Purdie Treloar (Lord Mayor 1906-07) to raise funds for a school and college for disabled children. The Lord Mayor continues to be a trustee of the school; each year the Lord Mayor and Sheriffs visit Treloar's School, as do the Masters of many Livery Companies that continue to provide charitable support.

Livery Schools Link

The Livery Schools Link is a voluntary body that co-ordinates Livery Company support for schools in the Greater London area, ranging from one-off projects to long-term partnerships, all aimed at developing the skills for work and life among young people.

Every year the Livery Schools Link hosts a careers showcase, which exhibits the diverse range of trades, crafts and professions represented by the Livery. This event is usually coordinated with the London Careers Festival (LCF) and takes place in Guildhall.

Examination, Awarding and Training

Several Companies are directly involved in examination or training, awarding professional or academic qualifications. A few examples among many: Master of Wines awarded by the Vintners; Master Farrier awarded by the Farriers; various optical technician qualifications awarded by the Spectacle Makers; and diploma qualifications in medicine awarded by the Society of Apothecaries.

A tour of all the Livery Company websites reveals that at over 90 of the Companies retain substantive links with their trade, craft or profession through education. As new Companies form, they will no doubt continue and strengthen this tradition. The Livery Companies also maintain their links with vocational training and examination through the City & Guilds of London Institute; 18 seats on the Institute's governing council are reserved for the Livery Companies.

Gresham College

Gresham College is funded by a bequest left by Sir Thomas Gresham (Mercer) that the Mercers' Company and the City of London Corporation jointly administer. Since 1991 the College is in Barnard's Inn, although the reach of its lectures has been vastly extended by publication on YouTube. The President of Gresham College is the Lord Mayor.

University Bursaries and Scholarships

Several Livery Companies provide bursaries, scholarships or other forms of funding to support students and academics at university. A few examples include: the Distillers' Company, which awards a scholarship to an MSc student at Heriot-Watt University; the Engineers' Company, which supports engineering students who are suffering financial hardship; the Air Pilots Company, which awards four annual bursaries for the City

University aviation safety and management MSc courses; and the Marketors' Company, which funds a full-time MBA student at the Cass Business School. Many other Companies award prizes or contribute towards the cost of research and study at various UK universities.

The Armourers' & Brasiers' Company not only funds research and education in materials science, primarily at post-graduate level, but also invests in start-up businesses launched by some of the brightest scientists and engineers who have been supported by the Company in their studies.

The City's Support for Youth Organisations

The Livery Companies maintain strong links with youth organisations, in particular the Cadet Forces. Examples of Companies include the Tax Advisers, which are affiliated with the City of London Army Cadet Force; the Environmental Cleaners, which supports 75 Detachment Army Cadet Force based in south-east London; the Glovers and 444 (Shoreditch) Squadron Air Training Corps; the Haberdashers and 1475 Squadron Air Training Corps; the Coachmakers and Hornchurch Sea Cadets, to name but a few.

Some Livery Companies support Combined Cadet Forces units that are hosted by a school, such as the Cadets of St Dunstan's College, which are affiliated with the Marketors' Company, a relationship founded by Past Master Marketor Alderman and Sheriff Sir Paul Judge.

In 2011 at least 101 Cadet Forces units (up from 57 in 2006) were supported by City Livery Companies to provide mentoring, work placement, education and training opportunities, sponsoring awards, and to introduce Cadets to the City. The Reserve Forces & Cadets Association of Greater London is responsible for all the military input into the Lord Mayor's Show, an event in which many Cadet Forces units participate each year. The links between the Livery and the cadets are summarised in an annual newsletter, aptly titled 'Cadet Link', published by the Greater London Reserve Forces and Cadets' Association.

Several Livery Companies have also adopted St John Ambulance Cadet units, such as the Drapers' Company and its affiliation with St John Ambulance[9] Harold Hill Division. In recent times

---

[9] The first public duty conducted by St John Ambulance was the Lord Mayor's Show of 1886, although officially St John Ambulance recognises Queen Victoria's Golden Jubilee of 1887 as its first 'official' public duty.

one of the Lord Mayor's ADCs was found from along the leadership of St John Ambulance.

The City of London has only one Scout Group, founded in 1908 and believed to be the second Scout Group formed in England following Baden-Powell's experimental Camp on Brownsea Island and the publication of fortnightly instalments of 'Scouting for Boys'.

In 1910 the Court of Aldermen resolved that the 1st City of London Boy Scouts could append the words 'Lord Mayor's Own' to their title. It is now one of the largest Scout Groups in London. As with St John Ambulance, the Lord Mayor may also appoint an ADC from among the adult leadership of the Scout Association.

The Provincial Guilds

Many towns and cities around the UK still have Guilds (sometimes known as Gilds or Guildries) and several of these provincial Guilds have connections with the City of London and its Livery Companies.

In particular, the Company of Cutlers in Hallamshire (Sheffield) has a connection with the Worshipful Company of Cutlers, and the Shrewsbury Drapers' Company has a connection with the Worshipful Company of Drapers. The Shrewsbury Drapers' Company has the benefit of its own hall in the town centre.

The cities of Chester, Durham, Newcastle and York have a number of extant Guilds, the latter including the Company of Merchant Adventurers of the City of York; The York Butchers' Gild, which has links with the Worshipful Company of Butchers in London; and the Gild of Freemen of the City of York. The Cordwainers' Company maintains connections with its York brethren. The City of Bristol boasts its own Society of Merchant Venturers, and the City of Edinburgh has its own Company of Merchants.

Other cities in the UK with ancient Guilds include, among others: Aberdeen, Chester, Dundee, Exeter, Glasgow (with its 14 *Trades Houses*), Lincoln, Stirling, and Oxford. A more recent creation is the Worshipful Livery Company of Wales based in Cardiff, styled on a City of London Livery Company.

In total there are over 220 extant Guilds in the UK not including various associations of Freemen in towns and cities where Freemen are still admitted. One such example of a City that admits Freemen but has no surviving Guilds is Norwich. Since admitting women in 2010 the Freemen of Norwich has grown its numbers substantially and celebrated 700 years in 2017

The Glaziers' Company has published a booklet about the provincial Guilds, with details in the bibliography. A list of over

220 existing Guilds, with links to their website (if any), is on the website supporting this guide, with details in the 'Online Resources' chapter.

Two Guilds remain in the Republic of Ireland: The Goldsmiths' Company of Dublin which has premises in the Dublin Castle complex and runs the Assay Office for the Republic and the Apothecaries' Company which used to have a hall on Merrion Square in Dublin but since 2011 has been co-located with the Royal College of Physicians of Ireland on Kildare Street

Beyond the shores of the British Isles, two Companies in the United States of America have substantive links with their London counterparts, specifically the Honourable Cordwainers' Company and the Company of Carpenters of the City and County of Philadelphia. Several City of London Livery Companies are also connected with Guilds (or Zünfte) in Switzerland.

British merchants also setup similar structures in other countries to facilitate trade such as the English Factory (a 'factor' is an company's agent) in Porto. This organisation is comprised of the heads of the various British Port Wine shipping families that have dominated the trade for centuries and continue to this day.

The Feitoria Inglesa (English Factory) on Rua do Infanta D. Henrique was opened in 1790 and remains the home of the British Port Wine Trade in Portugal.

Online Resources

Numerous other information sources are available from Guildhall, the Museum of London, the various Livery Companies, Guilds, and City Companies without Livery. Some of the key information sources are signposted below:

- This guide is supported by a blog that provide links to a wealth of additional web-based resources, including photographs, a recommended reading list, and an associated YouTube channel that brings together all the best Gresham College lectures and videos about the City of London and its Livery Companies: cityandlivery.blogspot.co.uk

- The City of London Corporation's website page about the Livery provides a link to the A-Z of Livery Company contact details, and to the Livery Committee City Briefings booking pages, among much else: www.cityoflondon.gov.uk/livery

- The Livery Committee's website provides a wealth of resources for Masters, Clerks and civic officers on matters that span all the Livery Companies. It is also has its own database of Livery Company contacts: www.liverycommittee.org

- This Livery website complements much of the information in this Guide, together with Diary dates, links to many relevant websites, and background detail on the elections and other City ceremonial and livery customs: www.liverycompanies.info

- CityView and CityResident magazines are produced by the Corporation of London for business, city workers and residents. The magazines are available online at: www.cityoflondon.gov.uk/about-us/about-the-city-of-london-corporation/publications

- The Lord Mayor's Appeal outlines the rolling program of charitable initiative supported by the Lord Mayor of London: www.thelordmayorsappeal.org

- A list of every Livery Company, with a photograph of the Company's Master, a picture of the Master's Badge, location of the Company's Hall (if any) and a link to the Company's website are at: www.liverycompanies.com

- The Records of London's Livery Companies Online (ROLLCO) provides a searchable database of membership records of several Livery Companies since the 1400s. Here you can discover any ancestor who was an Apprentice, Freeman, Liveryman or even Master of one of the Companies currently enrolled in the database: www.londonroll.org

- The Proceedings of the Old Bailey is an online database of nearly 200,000 criminal trials held from 1674 to 1913: www.oldbaileyonline.org

- A searchable catalogue of the City of London libraries is at: col.ent.sirsidynix.net.uk

- A guide to the churches and other places of worship in the City of London: www.london-city-churches.org.uk/churchfinder.html

- The City of London Corporation online shop sells books, ties, cufflinks, brooches, and so on: https://shop.cityoflondon.gov.uk

- The Museum of London online collection of images related to the museum's exhibits, including many objects connected with the Livery Companies: collections.museumoflondon.org.uk/Online

- The London Metropolitan Archives has an extensive online catalogue and images database related to the City of London: collage.cityoflondon.gov.uk

- The Annual Sheep Drive hosted by the Woolmen's Company has a website with online booking: sheepdrive.london

- The City of London Corporation is responsible for cattle in Epping Forest and has developed a fenceless system to keep them within grazing areas. The whereabouts of the cattle can be monitored using the NoFence app available for mobile devices.

- A list of most of the Livery Company affiliations with HM Armed Forces: bit.ly/29cQQz5

- A map of the City of London immediately before the Great Fire, showing the Livery Halls, is at: mapoflondon.uvic.ca/map.htm

- The City Heritage Society's website provides a rich resource for exploring the past winners of the City Heritage Award https://cityheritage.org.uk/

- The Livery Companies Apprenticeship Scheme provides details of apprenticeship and the Livery Companies Skills Council's Master Certificate Scheme and the City & Guilds Professional Recognition Award: https://lcas.co.uk/

Most of the Livery Companies have an X (formerly Twitter) or Facebook account. The author follows all the Corporation of the City of London and Livery Company X accounts and tweets regular facts about the City and Livery with the hashtags #CityFact and #LiveryFact. A simple way to identify whether a Livery Company has a X account is to look at the list of accounts followed by @CityandLivery. The author also has a Facebook account at facebook.com/CityandLivery

If All Else Fails

The rich and complex history of the City of London and its diverse Livery Companies weave a colourful and gilded tapestry older still than the oldest Royal Charter granted to a Guild in England, aptly held by the Weavers' Company of London (1155). If you seek a simple, rational and complete view of the City then consider first the words of the Royal Commission into Local Government 1957-1960, otherwise known as the Herbert Commission:

> *Logic has its limits and the position of the City lies outside them.*

The very best and final advice available to those who seek the answer to the City is to be found in its own motto:

DOMINE DIRIGE NOS

which translates as 'Lord Direct Us'

or in Cockney as 'Gawd 'elp us!'

Appendix A - Masonic Lodges of the City Livery Companies

Several Livery Companies and other City institutions have associated Masonic Lodges. The following list identifies various lodges, with their date of formation, and associated Company or organisation if not obvious from the Lodge's name:

Pellipar Lodge, No. 2693 (1898) (Skinners' Company)
Cutlers' Lodge, No. 2730 (1898)
Guildhall Lodge, No. 3116
Guild of Freemen Lodge, No. 3525 (1911) (Freemen of the City)
St Catherine's Lodge, No. 3743 (1914) (Turners' Company)
City Livery Lodge, No. 3752 (1915) (General)
Feltmakers' Lodge, No. 3839 (1917)
Taurus Lodge, No. 3981 (1919) (Butchers' Company)
Corium Lodge, No. 4041 (1919) (Leather Industry)
Paynters Stainers Lodge, No. 4256 (1921)
Needlemakers' Lodge, No. 4343 (1921)
Tekton Lodge, No. 4696 (1924) (Carpenters' Company)
Laus Deo Lodge, No. 4821 (1926) (Bakers' Company)
Lora Et Aries Lodge, No. 5086 (1929) (Loriners' Company)
Lodge of St Julian, No. 5107 (1929) (Innholders' Company)
Basketmakers' Lodge, No. 5639 (1936)
Paviors' Lodge, No. 5646 (1936)
Lodge of Love and Friendship, No. 6123 (1946) (Gold and Silver Wyredrawers' Company)
Farriers' Lodge, No. 6305 (1946)
Poulters' Lodge, No. 6876 (1949)
Blacksmiths' Lodge, No. 7175 (1952)
Plaisterers' Lodge, No. 7390 (1955)
City of London Lodge of Installed Masters, No. 8220 (1968)[10]
Per Caelum Lodge, No. 8602 (1974) (Air Pilots)

---

[10] Formed for Installed Masters of Lodges who are (a) in a City Livery Lodge, (b) who are members of City Livery Companies, (c) who are members of the City Corporation.

Lodge of St Paul's Wharf, No. 8731 (1976) (Carmen)
Tergere Lodge, No. 8830 (1978) (Environmental Cleaners)
Cito Lodge, No. 9650 (1997) (Information Technologists)
City Gate Lodge, No. 9890 (2013) (Security Professionals)

Pellipar Lodge is the oldest, and most senior. It was consecrated in the Cedar Drawing Room of Skinners' Hall in February 1898. All the founders were members of the Skinners' Company.

It should be noted that these Masonic Lodges are separate institutions from the Livery Companies from which they draw their membership. Not every Livery Company has a Masonic Lodge, neither are all Freemen or Liverymen members of Freemasonry.

There is no requirement to be a Freemason in order to join a Livery Company and progress to the office of Master, Prime Warden or Upper Bailiff. Freemasonry and the Livery Companies are separate organisations that happen to share some members in common.

Appendix B - Dress for City Dinners and Banquets

The man who can dominate a London dinner table can dominate the world.

Oscar Wilde

Three dress codes are typically observed for City banquets, lunches and other social occasions. They are White Tie (evening tails), sometimes described as 'formal'; Black Tie (dinner jacket), sometimes described as 'semi-formal'; and Morning Dress. Increasingly those events where Morning Dress is worn also permit dark lounge suits (business attire). Casual dress or sports clothing may be appropriate for other events. We shall concern ourselves with those events where a higher standard of dress is expected.

In all instances, the final word on appropriate dress lies with the organisation hosting the event, and subtle differences in dress code might exist from one Company to another. Serving members of HM Armed Forces and senior Police and Fire Service officers in the UK and Commonwealth Realms are often encouraged to wear mess dress with medals, and gentlemen with Scottish ancestral lineage may wear Highland or Lowland dress. There is even a City of London tartan for those who wish to wear it. The design is based on the colours of the City's coat of arms and was registered in 2012:

www.tartanregister.gov.uk (search for City of London)

Clerics have their own dress code, which does not echo the marshal origins of certain aspects of black and white tie, especially in respect of the absence of braids down the legs of gentlemen's black and white tie trousers.

Ladies should dress in a manner that is appropriate to the occasion. Ladies have a far wider choice of colour and style of dress than the gentlemen, and ladies are not expected to dress in black. In general ladies should wear long dresses covering their shoulders. Gloves and tiaras may occasionally be worn for the most formal of events. A simple rule of thumb applies: the greater the effort of the host, the greater the level of formality expected of the guest.

Note: A dinner is generally of three courses, whereas a banquet has four or more courses. Preprandial drinks are invariably served before dinners and banquets, a stirrup cup will usually follow dinner.

Evening Dress (White Tie)

This is the most formal dress code and is usually reserved for the most important of City and Livery Company events, such as the annual Lord Mayor's Banquet or a Livery Company partners' dinner, or most Mansion House banquets.

For gentlemen:

- A black or midnight blue evening tailcoat
- Matching black or midnight blue evening trousers with two parallel lines of braid down the outer side of each leg.
- A white evening shirt, with winged collar, ideally with a plain starched front, buttons and cufflinks (see note)
- A white bow tie, ideally of the type you tie yourself
- A white adjustable evening waistcoat
- Black shoes, highly polished
- Black socks

Strict interpretations of White Tie also include a top hat, cape, white gloves, a white scarf and optionally a cane. Whilst acceptable and correct, these items along with spats might be considered overkill.

Note: Each Livery Company has its own insignia, possibly including cufflinks with the Company coat of arms.

For ladies:

Although female dress is not as formally codified as that of gentlemen, ladies are expected to wear full-length dresses. Dresses with lengths above the ankle (such as cocktail or tea-length dresses) are considered inappropriate. Shoulders should be covered with a stole or a shawl.

Depending on the formality of the event, long gloves are a possible accessory. Women's gloves should be white and upper-length/opera-length and are never taken off until seated at a table. Then they are worn again after the meal is finished. Evening shoes or pumps are essential, together with appropriate hosiery and a matching evening bag.

Colour is a matter of personal choice; most formal evening dresses are single-colour and the variation and decoration comes from beads or patterns in the fabric. The dress should be appropriate to, and consistent with, the event.

Best jewellery should be worn; the key is to aim for shimmer rather than extravagance. Where state decorations are worn it is also appropriate to wear a tiara (married women and widows only), although this is becoming less common except for very formal state occasions.

Black Tie

This is a semi-formal dress code and often used for less formal dinners in the City. Nowadays Black Tie is used for many dinners in the City, and in a few cases may be worn at White Tie events, although confirmation should always be sought from the hosting organisation.

For gentlemen:

- A black or midnight blue dinner jacket, or black velvet smoking jacket
- Black or midnight blue dinner trousers with one line of braid down the outer side of each leg.
- A white evening shirt with a fold down collar (never a wing collar), ideally with a Marcella front and either studs or buttons
- A black bow tie, ideally of the type you tie yourself
- Black shoes, highly polished
- Black socks

Note: Good-quality evening shirts also require collar stiffeners.

Some Companies permit the wearing of black waistcoats, whilst others discourage it. As always, it is best to check with the hosting organisation, if in doubt.

The strictest interpretation of Black Tie requires slightly different trousers than those worn for White Tie, with the latter having two lines of braid down each leg compared with one line of braid for Black Tie. In practice the distinction is rarely adhered to.

For ladies:

Dresses appropriate for Black Tie are either floor-length or a three-quarter-length evening gown. A long dress or skirt remains the safest option appropriate to any Black Tie event grander than a cocktail party. The dress should be appropriate to the event and will normally be a single colour with beading or patterns forming the interest. A simple black dress is always appropriate, with jewellery, shoes and bag providing the highlight.

Best jewellery should be worn, such as sparkly earrings and bracelet or simple button earrings and a simple gold or silver necklace.

Morning Dress

The various Ward Clubs and the City Livery Club still adhere to the practice of wearing Morning Dress for their respective annual civic luncheons. Purists will also insist on Morning Dress for the election of the Lord Mayor and Sheriffs at Common Hall. This dress code is similar to that worn by gentlemen at smarter weddings and the Ascot races but with a strong suggestion of black coats and waistcoats.

For gentlemen:

- A dark grey morning coat worn with a black waistcoat
- Striped grey trousers (Cashmere stripes)
- A plain white shirt with a fold down or winged collar
- A tie of sober colour or pattern (Livery, club, or regimental ties are now deemed acceptable)
- Black shoes, highly polished
- Black socks

For ladies:

An appropriate daytime dress and hat as one might wear to a wedding or church service. Gloves and a long coat may optionally be worn depending on the weather.

Livery Badges, Sashes, Medals, Spurs and Decorations

Many City and Livery Company dinners specifying White Tie or Black Tie will invite members to wear Livery badges, sashes, medals and crown or diplomatic decorations. In the case of Livery sashes, badges and medals the wearer will know if they have these items of insignia and are hence entitled to wear them. Livery medals should always be worn on the right-hand side.

Military medals should be worn in accordance with the customs and regulations for wearing them. Those members of HM Armed

Forces permitted to wear spurs may do so with mess dress. The same guidance applies to medals awarded to members of the Emergency Services and St John Ambulance.

Some Livery Companies still stipulate that guests should only wear badges of office when invited *ex officio*, such as in the capacity of a Master, rather than as a personal guest. Wearing of gongs when not required can be construed as being *infra dig*.

Decorations refer to Crown Honours such as the collars, sashes and badges of orders of chivalry. Under no circumstances should collars, sashes, medals or decorations be worn that the Sovereign has not legitimately awarded to the wearer. Decorations conferred on a UK citizen from a foreign state should be worn only with the explicit permission of the Crown.

The Royal British Legion publishes advice on the etiquette of wearing military medals awarded to deceased family members, and generally they should be worn only by widows or widowers on the right breast at appropriate events such as national events of commemoration.

Appendix C - City Etiquette

The citizens of London are universally renowned and talked about for their superiority over those of other cities in the refinement of their dress, manners, and dining.

William Fitzstephen, late 12th century.

The complexity of the City of London and Livery Company customs, ceremonies and hierarchy of officers can be confusing and impenetrable. This may especially be the case for guests attending formal dinners, banquets and other events for the first time.

Whilst a full exploration of the subject of etiquette is beyond the scope of this appendix, the following general advice should suffice for most formal events.

Addressing the Host

The host should always be addressed by the title of their office when in public, such as Lord Mayor, Lord Mayor Locum Tenens, Sheriff, Master, Prime Warden, Upper Bailiff. This simple etiquette should be adhered to even when the incumbent is a close personal friend.

Dress Code

The dress code for formal events will be communicated on the invitation and repeated on any *Pour Mémoire* card sent to persons who are confirmed to attend. Adherence to the dress code is considered good manners.

The Loyal Toast

When the Loyal Toast is called, all diners stand and sing the first verse of the National Anthem; thereafter the toast is 'The King' before drinking.

The Toast to the Royal Family

When the toast to the Royal Family is called, all diners stand and the first few bars of the National Anthem might be played but diners do not sing. The toast is 'The Royal Family'.

The Civic Toast

Most events will involve a toast to The Lord Mayor and the City of London Corporation, or (if the Sheriffs are present) The Lord Mayor, Sheriffs and the City of London Corporation. This can be quite a mouthful and the author believes it is acceptable, if not precisely correct, to respond simply with 'The Lord Mayor'.

Punctuality

Livery Company formal events adhere to strict timings that should be observed. It is a discourtesy to the host to be late.

Leaving the Table

Unless there is a medical emergency, you should remain seated throughout the meal at least up until the Loyal Toast, although a comfort break is often announced before the speeches begin.

Mobile Phones

All mobile phones and other electronic devices should be silenced during the formal proceedings. A few discreet photographs taken before the top table is seated may be acceptable.

Smoking

Mansion House and Guildhall do not permit smoking anywhere on the premises. Livery Company Halls invariably are smoke-free premises unless a special 'port and cigars' event is organised. It is best to proceed on the assumption that smoking is not permitted.

Speeches and Presentations

Silence should be observed during all speeches, presentations or other entertainment (such as a poetry recital or musical piece) with the exception of background music. Applause is appropriate at the end of speeches, when an award has been presented, or at the end of a musical interlude, except where a Grace is sung before or after dinner.

Topics of Conversation

Personal relationships, religion and politics are topics of conversation best avoided during Livery Company events. The accomplished deipnosophist will ensure they speak to all those seated to their left and right side as well as to those opposite, actively listening as well as speaking.

Guests

The behaviour of guests is the responsibility of the Livery Company member who has invited them, and it is the host member's responsibility to brief them on matters of etiquette, this is especially important for those guests who are prospective members of a Livery Company.

The Loving Cup

Every Livery Company banquet will include a Loving Cup ceremony and it is one in which all diners participate. The ceremony will usually be explained prior to being demonstrated, it is best not to try and take it too seriously and rather just go with the flow. Diners are not required to drink from the cup if they do not wish to do so.

The Stirrup Cup

The most formal of City events usually finishes with an invitation to join the Master for a stirrup cup, which means an after-dinner drink. There is no obligation to attend and it is entirely acceptable to depart during the stirrup cup. It is not necessary to linger to say goodnight to the Master unless the opportunity arises or you are a personal guest or close relative of the Master.

Gratuities

Under no circumstances should any employee of a Livery Company or member of staff employed by a catering or events contractor be tipped. If a person has gone out of their way to be helpful, it is best to mention this to the Clerk. It is appropriate to leave a few coins in a tray provided for that purpose with the cloakroom staff.

Security at Mansion House

Diners attending a formal event at Mansion House should anticipate a brief, but important, security check on arrival at the Walbrook Hall entrance. Occasionally it will be necessary to bring a form of photo ID in addition to an invitation card. Please check the invitation for details.

Appendix D - Please Pass the Port

No Livery Company dinner or banquet would be complete without the serving of a good-quality vintage port, Madeira, brandy or dessert wine before the Loyal Toast. Sometimes the wine will be served in a decanter, in which case all the diners have a role to play since it is they rather than the catering staff who pass around the decanter.

Various customs associated with the port service have arisen to ensure that the decanter circulates among the diners so they all get equal opportunity to share in its contents. If you follow these simple rules you won't go wrong:

1. Always pass the port to the diner to your left, or as they say in the Royal Navy 'Port to port'.

The decanter is placed at the end of your table or 'sprig', adjacent to the host or whomsoever is seated at the top table end of a sprig. In the event of particularly long sprigs, a decanter may be placed at either end, each proceeding down one side of the sprig.

No matter where the decanters are initially placed, they always pass to the left (clockwise on a round table) and continue to circulate until empty. Diners who do not wish to partake pass the decanter onward to the left.

2. Encourage your fellow diners to pass the port.

In the unthinkable event that a fellow diner allows the decanter to settle upon the table at their position, a polite way to invite them to continue passing the port is to ask the errant diner 'Do you know the Bishop of Norwich?'.

A seasoned diner would detect the mild rebuke in this question, and humbly and swiftly pass on the decanter. For others, the response to this question is usually 'No I don't, do tell me more?' (or words to that effect), in which case you can reply 'Oh, he was an awfully nice fellow, but he rarely passed the port'. This is said to derive from a past Bishop of Norwich who used to fall asleep at dinners, perhaps in part because of his prodigious consumption of port, whereupon the decanters would all come to rest in front of him to the annoyance of his fellow diners.

The other possibility is that your guest does know the incumbent Bishop of Norwich, in which case you had better have an amusing story to tell about The Right Reverend.

Another option is to ask your guest a more direct question such as 'Have you got an up-to-date pass....port?'

3. Do not allow the decanter to touch the table (if customary).

Some Livery Companies and Regiments of the British and Commonwealth Armed Forces observe the custom that the decanter should not touch the table, further ensuring that the decanter does not settle with a diner (unless they wish to hold it aloft for the evening). Whether your Company practices this custom should be confirmed with the Clerk.

To facilitate this custom, the Hoggit decanter was invented. It features a rounded base that can be seated only in a custom-made wooden foot that resides with the host. The decanter would tip over if placed on the table, thus ensuring that it continues to circulate.

4. Wait until the Loyal Toast

The port is served before the Loyal Toast, and in sufficient time to allow it to circulate fully among all the diners before the Loyal Toast is called. It is exceptionally bad form to drink the port before the Loyal Toast. Diners who do not wish to drink port may participate in the Loyal Toast (and subsequent toasts) with wine or water.

Appendix E - Selected City Ceremonies

Sir John Cass Service (Red Feather Day)
St Botolph Aldgate
January or February

The Golden Lecture
St Bartholomew the less
March

The Trial of the Pyx
Goldsmiths' Hall
February - May

The Spital Sermon
St Lawrence Jewry
March - April

United Guilds' Service
St Paul's Cathedral
Almost always two Fridays before Good Friday

John Stow Commemoration Service
St Andrew Undershaft
On or near 5th April (every third year)

Knollys Rose Ceremony
Seething Lane to Mansion House
On or near 22nd June

Cart Marking Ceremony
Guildhall Yard
On or near 19th July

Swan Upping
River Thames, Sunbury - Abingdon
Third week in July

Doggett's Coat and Badge Wager
London Bridge to Chelsea
July or August

Admission of Sheriffs
Guildhall
Late September

Christ's Hospital St Matthew's Day Parade
Guildhall Yard
Late September (usually close to 21st)

Sheep Drive (only Freemen and a nominated guest may
participate)
London Bridge
Third Sunday in September

Election of the Lord Mayor (Common Hall)
Guildhall
Michaelmas Day, 29th September (or nearest weekday)

The Lion Sermon
St Katharine Cree, Leadenhall
13:00 on 16th October or next nearest weekday

Quit Rents Ceremony
The Royal Courts of Justice
October

The Silent Ceremony (Admission of The Lord Mayor elect)
Guildhall
Friday before the second Saturday in November

The Lord Mayor's Show
Mansion House to Royal Courts of Justice
Second Saturday in November

Festival of St Cecilia
Wednesday nearest to 22nd November

Rotates annually between St Paul's Cathedral, Westminster Abbey and Westminster Cathedral

Presentation of a Boar's Head to the Lord Mayor
by The Butchers Company
Mansion House
On or near 6th December (Feast of St Nicholas)

Gun Salutes
62 rounds are fired by the Honourable Artillery Company
HM Tower of London on the Sovereign's Birthdays (actual and official), the Birthday of the Sovereign's wife or consort, the Birthday of the Prince of Wales, Accession Day, Coronation Day.

41 volleys are fired during visits by Foreign Heads of State.

Note: On occasions when late Duke of Edinburgh's birthday coincided with the weekend of Trooping the Colour (the Sovereign's official birthday), the Honourable Artillery Company fired a record-breaking 124 rounds from HM Tower of London.

Appendix F - Livery Companies and Guilds with their Churches

The following table lists all the current Livery Companies in order of precedence with their associated Guild Church. Many of these Companies are styled *The Worshipful Company of...* except the Master Mariners and the Air Pilots, both of which are styled *The Honourable Company of...* and the Apothecaries, which is styled *The Worshipful Society of...*

Precedence	Company	Guild Church
1	Mercers*	St Andrew by the Wardrobe
2	Grocers*	St Mary-le-Bow, St Stephen Walbrook
3	Drapers*	St Michael Cornhill
4	Fishmongers*	St Magnus the Martyr
5	Goldsmiths*	St Vedast Alias Foster
6/7	Skinners*	St James Garlickhythe
7/6	Merchant Taylors*	St Helen's Bishopsgate
8	Haberdashers*	St Lawrence Jewry
9	Salters*	None, but frequently St James Cripplegate
10	Ironmongers*	St Botolph without Aldgate
11	Vintners*	St James Garlickhythe
12	Clothworkers*	St Olave Hart Street
13	Dyers*	St James Garlickhythe
14	Brewers*	None

15	Leathersellers*	St Botolph without
16	Pewterers*	St Vedast Alias Foster
17	Barbers*	St Giles Cripplegate
18	Cutlers*	St Martin-within-Ludgate
19	Bakers*	All Hallows by the Tower
20	Wax Chandlers*	St Vedast Alias Foster
21	Tallow Chandlers*	None
22	Armourers and Brasiers*	St Margaret Lothbury
23	Girdlers*	St Lawrence Jewry
24	Butchers*	St Bartholomew the Great
25	Saddlers*	St Vedast Alias Foster
26	Carpenters*	All Hallows by the Tower, Dutch Church, Austin Friars
27	Cordwainers	St Dunstan in the West
28	Painter-Stainers*	St James Garlickhythe
29	Curriers	St Michael Paternoster Royal
30	Masons	None
31	Plumbers	St Magnus the Martyr
32	Innholders*	St Michael Paternoster Royal
33	Founders*	St Bartholomew the Great
34	Poulters	St Peter upon Cornhill
35	Cooks	St Botolph without Aldersgate

36	Coopers*	St Botolph without
37	Tylers and Bricklayers	St Margaret Lothbury
38	Bowyers	None
39	Fletchers*	St Bartholomew the Great
40	Blacksmiths	St Andrew by the Wardrobe
41	Joiners and	St James Garlickhythe
42	Weavers	St James Garlickhythe
43	Woolmen	St Michael Cornhill
44	Scriveners	St Martin-within-Ludgate
45	Fruiterers	St Mary Abchurch
46	Plaisterers*	St Vedast Alias Foster
47	Stationers and Newspaper Makers*	St Bride's
48	Broderers	None
49	Upholders	St Michael Cornhill
50	Musicians	St Sepulchre without Newgate
51	Turners	St Bride's
52	Basketmakers	St Margaret Pattens
53	Glaziers and Painters of Glass*	Southwark Cathedral
54	Horners	St James Garlickhythe
55	Farriers	None

56	Paviors	St Martin-within-Ludgate
57	Loriners	St Lawrence Jewry
58	Apothecaries*	St Andrew by the Wardrobe
59	Shipwrights	None
60	Spectacle Makers	St Bride's
61	Clockmakers	St James Garlickhythe
62	Glovers	St Margaret Lothbury
63	Feltmakers	St Bartholomew the Great
64	Framework Knitters	St Peter's Oadby
65	Needlemakers	St James Garlickhythe
66	Gardeners	St Giles Cripplegate
67	Tin Plate Workers	St Margaret Lothbury
68	Wheelwrights	None
69	Distillers	St Lawrence Jewry
70	Pattenmakers	St Margaret Pattens
71	Glass Sellers	St James Garlickhythe
72	Coachmakers and Coach Harness Makers	St James Garlickhythe
73	Gunmakers*	None
74	Gold and Silver Wyre Drawers	St James Garlickhythe

75	Makers of Playing Cards	None
76	Fanmakers	St James Garlickhythe
77	Carmen*	St Michael Paternoster Royal
78	Master Mariners*	St Michael Cornhill
79	City of London Solicitors' Company	St Peter ad Vincula
80	Farmers*	St Bartholomew the Great
81	Air Pilots	St Michael Cornhill
82	Tobacco Pipe Makers and Tobacco Blenders	St Lawrence Jewry
83	Furniture Makers*	St Mary-le-Bow
84	Scientific Instrument Makers*	St Margaret Lothbury
85	Chartered Surveyors	St Lawrence Jewry
86	Chartered Accountants in England and Wales	St Martin-within-Ludgate
87	Chartered Secretaries and Administrators	None

88	Builders' Merchants	St Peter ad Vincula
89	Launderers*	Southwark Cathedral
90	Marketors	St Bride's
91	Actuaries	St Lawrence Jewry
92	Insurers	St Lawrence Jewry
93	Arbitrators	St Mary-le-Bow
94	Engineers	St Peter ad Vincula, St Vedast Alias Foster
95	Fuellers	None
96	Lightmongers	St Botolph without Aldgate
97	Environmental Cleaners	St Olave Hart Street
98	Chartered Architects*	St Lawrence Jewry
99	Constructors	St Lawrence Jewry
100	Information Technologists*	St Bartholomew the Great
101	World Traders	All Hallows by the Tower
102	Water Conservators	St Michael Cornhill, St Mary-at-Hill
103	Firefighters	St Mary-le-Bow
104	Hackney Carriage Drivers	St Bartholomew the Great

105	Management Consultants	St Mary-le-Bow
106	International Bankers	St Mary-le-Bow
107	Tax Advisers	St Bartholomew the Great
108	Security Professionals	St Peter ad Vincula
109	Educators	St James Garlickhythe
110	Arts Scholars	St Peter ad Vincula
111	Nurses	

* These Companies own a hall, individually or jointly.

The following Guilds and City Companies without Livery will join the order of precedence based on their date of elevation to the status of Livery Company:

• The Company of Communicators
• The Company of Entrepreneurs
• The Company of Human Resource Professionals
• The Guild of Investment Managers

The Court of Aldermen also recognises two City Companies that will never progress to Livery Company status for reasons explained earlier in this guide:

• The Company of Watermen and Lightermen
• The Parish Clerks' Company

Appendix G - Livery Company Halls

The following Livery Companies have halls in the City of London, either individually or jointly owned:

Architects - Temple Bar EC4M 7DX
Apothecaries - Blackfriars Lane EC4V 6EJ
Armourers & Brasiers (Armourers' Hall) - 81 Coleman Street EC2R 5BJ
Bakers - 9 Harp Lane, EC3R 6DP
Barber-Surgeons* - 1 Monkwell Square EC2Y 5BL
Brewers - Aldermanbury Square EC2V 7HR
Butchers - 87 Bartholomew Close EC1A 7EB
Carmen - 186C Fleet St, EC4A 2HR
Carpenters - Throgmorton Avenue EC2N 2JJ
Clothworkers - Mincing Lane EC3R 7AH
Coopers - 13 Devonshire Square EC2M 4TH
Cutlers - Warwick Lane EC4M 7BR
Drapers - Throgmorton Avenue EC2N 2DQ
Dyers - 11-13 Dowgate Hill EC4R 2ST
Farmers & Fletchers - 3 Cloth Street EC1A 7LD
Fishmongers - London Bridge EC4R 9EL
Founders - Cloth Fair EC1A 7HT
Furniture Makers - 12 Austin Friars EC2 2HE
Girdlers - Basinghall Avenue EC2V 5DD
Glaziers, Scientific Instrument Makers, Launderers Hall - 9 Montague Close SE1 9DD
Goldsmiths - Foster Lane EC2V 6BN
Grocers - Princes Street EC2R 8AD
Haberdashers - 18 West Smithfield EC1A 9HQ
Information Technologists - 39a Bartholomew Close EC1 7JN
Innholders - College Street EC4R 2RH
Ironmongers - Barbican EC2Y 8AA
Leathersellers - St Helen's Place EC3A 6AB
Mercers - Ironmonger Lane EC2V 8HE
Merchant Taylors - 30 Threadneedle Street EC2R 8AY
Painter-Stainers (Painters' Hall) - 9 Little Trinity Lane EC4V 2AD
Pewterers - Oat Lane EC2V 7DE

Plaisterers - 1 London Wall EC2Y 5JU
Saddlers - 40 Gutter Lane EC2V 6BR
Salters - 4 Fore Street EC2Y 5DE
Skinners - 8½ Dowgate Hill EC4R 2SP
Stationers & Newspaper Makers - Ave Maria Lane EC4M 7DD
Tallow Chandlers - 4 Dowgate Hill EC4R 2SH
Vintners - 68 Upper Thames Street EC4V 3BG
Wax Chandlers - 6 Gresham Street EC2V 7AD

* Barber-Surgeons' Hall is the Livery hall of the Barbers' Company, which as one might reasonably infer from the City's love of anomaly, has a membership almost entirely composed of medical professionals and devoid of those with tonsorial talents.

One Company uses a hall owned by its respective professional body:

Accountants - 11 Copthall Avenue EC2R 7EF

One other Livery Company has a hall outside the City of London which is a working premises:

Gunmakers - 56 Commercial Road E1 1LP

One Company formed by Act of Parliament has a hall in the City of London:

Watermen and Lightermen (Watermen's Hall) - 16-18 St Mary-at-Hill, EC3R 8EF

Finally, the Guildhall complex includes a Livery hall. The hall was built between 1870 and 1873 with the intention of becoming a shared Livery Hall for those Livery Companies that had no hall of their own, yet none used it and the hall is now hired for various City functions.

Note: A photo book of the interiors of these Livery Halls was commissioned in 2018 by the Worshipful Company of Architects; see bibliography.

Appendix H - Sites of Former Halls

Several Livery Companies have occupied multiple halls in the City. Some have rebuilt on the same site several times. Others have relocated elsewhere in the City having been subject to compulsory purchase, been gifted properties or sold land. Many of the Livery Companies erected new premises following the Great Fire of London, during which 44 halls were burned, or after the Blitz when 16 halls were destroyed. Some of these sites are identified with a blue plaque.

The following is an incomplete list of former Livery Company halls on one or multiple sites:

Blacksmiths' Hall - Lambeth Hill / Queen Victoria St
Bowyers' Hall - Hart Street
Broderers' Hall - Gutter Lane
Coachmakers' Hall - Oat Lane
Cooks' Hall - Aldersgate Street
Coopers' Hall - Basinghall Street*
Cordwainers' Hall - St Paul's Churchyard, now Festival Gardens
Curriers' Hall - Cripplegate
Cutlers' Hall - Cloak Lane*
Dyers' Hall - Upper Thames St*
Fletchers' Hall - St Mary Axe*
Founders' Hall - Lothbury*
Framework Knitters' Hall - Whitecross Street
Fruiterers' Hall - Dowgate Hill
Glovers' Hall - Cromwell High Walk
Haberdashers' Hall - Gresham Street
Joiners and Ceilers' Hall - Upper Thames Street
Masons' Hall - Masons Avenue (a.k.a Masons Lane)
Master Mariners - HQS Wellington, Temple Stairs
Parish Clerks - Clerks Place, Broad Lane and Silver Street
Pinners' Hall - Old Broad Street
Plumbers' Hall - Bush Lane
Poulters' Hall - Butcher Lane (King Edward Street)
Turners' Hall - Philpott Lane and College Hill
Tylers and Bricklayers' Hall - Leadenhall Street

Uppholders' Hall - St Peter's Hill
Waterbearers' Hall - Bishopsgate
Weavers' Hall - Basinghall Street
Woodmongers' Hall - near Baynard's Castle

* These companies now own halls elsewhere in the City.

A book of pencil sketches of the Livery Halls as they were in 1904 is available for purchase on request from the Worshipful Company of Surveyors. The book is printed on demand by Lavenham Press and may be customised with a dedication of the purchaser's choice; see bibliography.

Note: The design of blue plaques in the City is different from elsewhere in England and their placement is regulated by the City of London Corporation rather than by English Heritage.

Appendix I - Livery Company Cutters

The Thames Traditional Rowing Association (TTRA) formed in 2003 counts the following Livery Companies and other City of London institutions among its membership, each having a cutter who participates in the various rowing challenges and river-based ceremonies such as the Lord Mayor's Flotilla on the morning of the Lord Mayor's Show.

TTRA Full Members:

Barbers
Drapers
Fishmongers
Founders
Glaziers
Information Technologists
Launderers
Master Mariners
Mercers
Scientific Instrument Makers (two cutters)
Tallow Chandlers
Water Conservators
Watermen and Lightermen
Wax Chandlers
Trinity House
Port of London Authority (two cutters)

TTRA Associate Members:

Bakers
Brewers
Carpenters
Coopers
Cutlers
Leathersellers
Poulters
Salters

Appendix J - City Heritage Awards

The following buildings have received the City Heritage Award jointly presented by the City Heritage Society and the Worshipful Company of Painter Stainers. The award takes form of a circular plaque, similar in dimensions to the iconic Blue Plaque seen outside the Square Mile. The City Heritage Award recognises architecture of note. In most years a single award is made, but on exceptional occasions a double award has been made in a single year.

Searching for the plaques and learning a little about the history and the characters connected with these buildings makes for an excellent self-guided tour of the City, though not necessarily in date order unless you were going to invest in a new soles for your shoes anyway.

Award Winners

1978 - 31 Newbury Street, adjacent to the Hand & Shears Pub
1979 - Porter Tun Room, 52 Chiswell Street
1980 - The Counting House (Union Discount Company), Cornhill
1981 - Cannons City Sporting Club
1982 - Fishmongers' Hall
1983 - Unilever House
1984 - 68-73 Cornhill
1985 - Magnesia House, 6 Playhouse Yard
1986 - Bengal Warehouse, 16A New Street
1987 - Clothworkers Hall
1988 - 41-43 Trinity Square and 6-7 Crescent
1989 - 13 Hayden Street (Cologne House) & Bank of England Museum
1990 - Lutyens House, Finsbury Circus
1991 - Rectory House
1992 - Royal Exchange and Bracken House, Cannon Street
1993 - Prudential Holborn Bars
1994 - Mansion House
1995 - East Meat Market, Smithfield
1996 - 1 Cornhill and 14 Brushfield Street

1997 - Lothbury Art Gallery
1998 - Counting House (2nd award), and 1-4 Middle Temple Lane
1999 - 71 Lombard Street
2000 - 41-42 Cloth Fair
2001 - Daily Express Building
2002 - Merrill Lynch, Newgate Street
2003 - Maugham Library
2004 - Rectory House, Lawrence Pountney Hill (2nd award).
2005 - Temple Bar and Barts Hospital
2006 - St Paul's Cathedral
2007 - 7 Lothbury
2008 - Unilever House (2nd award)
2009 - 1 Finsbury Circus
2010 - The Monument
2011 - 5,6,7 New Street, Bishopsgate
2012 - The Montcalm, 52 Chiswell Street
2013 - 4 Brabant Court
2014 - Holborn Viaduct Bridge and Holborn Viaduct Bridge N. E. Lodge
2015 - 8-10 Moorgate
2016 - Taylors Treasury, Bank of England.
2017 - Salters' Hall (Extension and refurbishment)
2018 - The Ned Hotel
2019 - 10 Trinity Square (the former Port of London Authority building) 2020 - 2023 No award owing to the Covid19 Pandemic which badly affected the Society. It expects to recommence awards in 2024.

Appendix K - Museums linked with the Livery

There are several museum outside of the City of London that have connections with the Livery Companies. The following incomplete list highlights some of the more notable collections:

The British Optical Association's Museum, Charing Cross. This small museum within the office of the British Optical Association contains a display relating the work of the Worshipful Company of Spectacle Makers.

The Stained Glass Museum, Ely Cathedral. This compact yet fascinating museum is tucked away inside Ely Cathedral. The museum has an extensive collection of stained glass showing the development of the craft through the ages. The museum is connected with the Glaziers' Company which has its own Stained Glass Repository (not open to the public).

The Weald and Download Living Museum, near Chichester. The Worshipful Company of Plumbers has a display of artefacts in this 'working' museum which showcases a wide range of crafts.

The Framework Knitters Museum at Ruddington records the development of the framework knitting machine and even has a gallery dedicated to Ned Ludd, leader of the Luddites!

The Fashion Museum in the Assembly Rooms, Bath is home to the collection of gloves loaned by the Worshipful Company of Glovers.

The Forge Mill Needle Museum, Redditch boasts a display of artefacts from the Needlemakers' Company. This small item belies the complexity of the processes involved in producing high quality needles for medical and other purposes.

The Chelsea Physic Garden, founded in 1673 is owned by the Society of Apothecaries. Access was limited for the first 310 years of the garden's existence but in 1983 it became a charitable trust and was opened to the public. The garden is the second oldest botanic garden in England and benefits from a shop and cafe.

The Horners' Company has an extensive collection on display in the Museum of design in Plastic located within the Arts University, Bournemouth. The Horners' Company is allied to the plastics industry which is the 21st century equivalent of horn.

Numerous other museums have received material support from one or more Livery Companies including but not limited to:

The Palace House Museum at Newmarket (Horse racing) to which the Saddlers' Company has donated several saddles.

The Ironbridge Gorge Museum which has received support from the Masons' Company and the Plumbers' Company.

The National Woollen Museum near Newcastle Emlyn in Carmarthenshire has received funding from the Clothworkers' Charity and the Worshipful Company of Weavers.

Appendix L - Idioms associated with the City and Livery Companies

Various phrases that are well known in the English language are likely to find their origins among the customs, ceremonies, and traditions of the City of London and its Livery Companies. The precise origin and veracity of these idioms can never be proven but they certainly have a long association with the City:

After the Lord Mayor's Show - a mundane end to an otherwise spectacular event, believed to refer to the sweeping up of horse dung left along the route of the Lord Mayor's Show.

At sixes and sevens - refers to the inability of the Skinners' and Merchant Taylors' companies to agree their position in the order of precedence.

Baker's Dozen - a quantity of thirteen (or less frequently fourteen) loaves sold as a 'dozen' awarded as a punishment to bakers who produced underweight good.

Keep it under your hat - believed to refer to the placement of the keys to the safe (wherein is kept the City's seal) in a pocket inside the hat of the City Swordbearer.

On Tenterhooks - referring to the specialised hooks that were used by the Clothworkers' Company to hold cloth under tension while drying out. Tenterhooks feature in the Company's arms.

If the cap fits, wear it - The Skinners Company elect their master by placing a cap on the head of each of the wardens of that company during the Cocks and Caps ceremony

There are many other words and sayings that are associated with City of London and Livery Company practices, some of them have their origins elsewhere and have become attached to the City, others find their origin in the Square Mile. See if you can find the link between the City and these words and sayings:

- Benchmark(ing)
- Bury the hatchet
- Copyright
- Hallmark(ing)
- Make your mark
- Past your prime
- Sent to Coventry
- Up to scratch
- Third Degree

Appendix L - Root & Branch Award Winners

HRH The Princess Royal speaking to the author on the occasion of the presentation of her Root & Branch Lifetime Achievement Award. Face masks were still necessary owing to the Covid 19 pandemic.

The following persons have received the City Livery Club's prestigious Root & Branch Award, which recognises exceptional service within and among the Livery. It is presented by the Lord Mayor of London. In some years the City Livery Club has also presented a Lifetime Achievement Award.

2014 Tom Ilube CBE
2014 Geoffrey Bond OBE (Lifetime Achievement Award)
2015 Phillip Davis
2016 Paul Jagger (the author)
2017 Keith Laurie
2017 Penrose Halson (Lifetime Achievement Award)
2018 Reginald Brown
2019 Peter French MBE

2019 Hugh Adams (Lifetime Achievement Award)
2020 - No award owing to the Covid19 Pandemic
2020 HRH The Princess Royal (Lifetime Achievement Award)*
2021 No award owing to the Covid19 Pandemic
2022 The Lifetime Kitchen Initiative
2022 Richard Humphries MBE (Lifetime Achievement Award)
2023 Michael Hockney MBE

* Award presented in 2021

The City Livery Club Root & Branch Award medal.

Appendix M - City Suppliers

The following list comprises some of the City supplier the author has either engaged directly, or enjoyed their services at events in the City:

The City Minstrel - Pianist, organist, composer and singer to the City Livery Companies   https://thecityminstrel.co.uk/

Gerald Sharp Photography - Photographer to City civic and Livery Company events https://sharpphoto.co.uk/

Fattorini - By Royal Appointment, manufacturers of Insignia Honours and Awards   https://fattorini.co.uk/

Newton Newton Flags - Flag and Banner maker https://newtonnewtonflags.com/

Life's Kitchen - Venue management, event management and catering   https://www.lifeskitchen.com/

Grant MacDonald - By Royal Appointment, Goldsmiths and Silversmiths   https://grantmacdonald.com/

The Cook & The Butler - City of London Event catering http://www.thecookandthebutler.co.uk/

Party Ingredients - Venue management, event management and catering   https://www.partyingredients.co.uk/

Digital Heraldry - Digital Heraldic Design and Artwork https://www.digitalheraldry.com/

Benson & Glegg - By Royal Appointment, suppliers of Buttons, Badges and Military Neckwear   https://bensonandclegg.com

City Posters

The following posters are available from cityandlivery.etsy.com or payhip.com/cityandlivery in both A2 colour print and digital download formats.

Map of Livery Halls

To enable further discovery and exploration, the author has commissioned a map of the City's Livery Halls, places of worship and other principal civic buildings (Mansion House, Guildhall, etc.) in the Square Mile. It features imagery of the frontage of each hall and iconography from the City's rich panoply of customs and traditions.

The map, commissioned by the author, illustrates the City's Livery Halls, places of worship and other principal civic buildings.

Elections and Appointments

The City Elections and Appointments poster shows how the City's government relates to the Residents, Business Voters, Freemen, the Livery Companies, and the Crown in a system of elections that remains essentially unchanged since the 12th century.

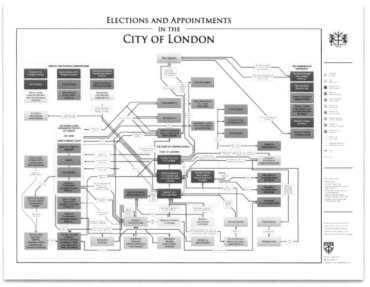

The infographic, commissioned by the author, of the Elections and Appointments in the City's sui generis system of government.

Arms of the City Companies

The City's Livery Companies and Companies without Livery boast the largest array of corporate heraldry in England. This poster illustrates the arms of all the companies presented in order of precedence. Many of these arms feature as pub signs throughout England.

This modern 'armorial roll', commissioned by the author, shows the coats of arms of all the City's Livery Companies and the two ancient companies without livery. Among them only one has not been lawfully granted by the Kings of Arms in London.

Glossary

Alderman - an elected officer in the City of London's upper chamber. One Alderman is elected for each of the 25 wards. The word imports either sex.

Alderwoman – some female Aldermen have chosen to style themselves as alderwomen, while the legal title remains Alderman.

Apprentice - a young person (school leaver) undergoing a period of occupational training, whilst in employment, under the supervision of a Freeman of the City of London. Modern apprenticeships last for a minimum of two years and involve a combination of formal education, occupational training, work placement and mentorship.

Armiger - a person who has a coat of arms either granted to them or inherited from their father.

Beadle (of a Company) - a paid officer of a Livery Company employed as a Master of Ceremonies and guardian of its possessions.

Beadle (of a ward) - an elected officer of a ward who performs ceremonial duties in support of the Alderman.

Chamberlain - a senior salaried officer of the City of London Corporation who performs the role of chief finance officer.

Chaplain - a honorary appointment, usually but not always held by an Anglican Priest, who provides advice, guidance and pastoral support to a Livery Company and its membership.

Clerk - the senior paid officer of a Livery Company, responsible for the efficient day-to-day running of the Company.

Coat of Arms - an arrangement of divisions and symbols (known as charges) on a shield, surmounted by a helm and crest which is granted by Letters Patent to a single person and their heirs or to a body corporate.

Common Council - the chamber of 100 elected members of the City of London Corporation.

Common Councilman - an elected officer in the City of London's lower chamber. Two or more Councilmen are elected for each of the 25 wards. The term imports either sex.

Common Hall - an assembly of the Liverymen of the several Livery Companies called for the purpose of electing the Lord Mayor, Sheriffs and certain other officers.

Court (of a Company) - the governing body of a Livery Company, equivalent to the board of directors.

Crest (on top of a Coat of Arms) – that part of a Coat of Arms which is on top of a helmet, placed above the shield. The word crest is sometime erroneously used to mean the whole coat of arms. If you think of a Coat of Arms as a car, the Crest is a roof-rack, the latter is affixed to the top of the former.

Fine - a fee levied on admission into the Freedom of the City of London. Also applies to fees levied on members of a Livery Company at each stage of their progression (admission into the Freedom, Livery, Court, Assistant, Wardens, etc).

Freedom - the status of being admitted into a Livery Company or the City of London, historically an important rite of passage for those who wished to trade in the City. Being a Freeman the City of London is still required for elected office and progression to Liveryman.

Freeman (of the City) - a person who has been admitted into the Freedom of a City after making a declaration. There are three routes to becoming a Freeman: by Patrimony, Redemption and Servitude (see below). The word imports either sex.

Freeman (of a Company) - a person who has been admitted into a Livery Company. The word imports either sex.

Journeyman - a qualified practitioner in a trade, craft or profession who is undergoing a period of professional development by rotating through assignments with multiple clients or employers. The word is not consistently applied across all the Livery Companies. The word imports either sex.

Letters Patent – a legal instrument in the form of document that is open for all to read, such as a Royal Charter or a Grant of Arms (Coat of Arms). These will often be on display in Livery Halls.

Lieutenant - A member of the City's Commission of Lieutenancy, appointed by His Majesty the King. There is no Lord Lieutenant in the City of London, rather the office is held in commission (i.e. by a group of people). The Lord Mayor of London is the chairman of the commission.

Livery Company - an occupational Guild in the City of London. One whose senior members participate in the election of the Lord Mayor, Sheriffs and certain other ancient officers. Livery companies are ranked in a strict order of precedence and are active in philanthropy, education, fellowship and support to their respective trade, craft or profession. Some retain regulatory, inspection, examination or other powers to uphold trading standards. Livery Companies maintain close bonds with the Armed Forces of the Crown and the Church of England.

Livery - a collective noun for the senior members of the Livery Companies and sometimes used to refer to the Livery Companies; also the robes worn by Liverymen of those Companies.

Liveryman - a senior member of a Livery Company, the grade from which the members of the Court are drawn. The word imports either sex.

Master - the presiding officer of a Livery Company Court and the senior Liveryman of the Company. Elected from among the members of the Company's Court, usually for a one-year term (except the Master Bowyer who serves two years). May also be titled Prime Warden or Upper Bailiff (of the Weavers). The word imports either sex.

Mother Company - the Livery Company into which a Freeman was first admitted.

Patrimony - the system by which a Freeman's children may become Freemen of the City of London if either of their parents were Freemen before they were born.

Redemption - the system by which admission to a Livery Company is obtained on payment of a fine and fulfilment of the Company's other membership criteria.

Servitude - the system by which an Apprentice may become a Freeman of the City of London on completion of a period of apprenticeship under the supervision of a Freeman.

Sheriff - an elected officer in the City of London exercising royal authority and first recorded in the 7th century. Nominally responsible for protecting Her Majesty's judges.

Supporters (Heraldry) – the animals, mythical beasts or persons placed either side of a Coat of Arms, supporting the shield. Supporters are granted only to the most eminent persons (peers of the realm, members of the royal family, knights of the Garter or Thistle) and to Royal Charter corporations such as a Livery Company.

Quarterage - the annual subscription fee levied by many Livery Companies upon their Freemen and Liverymen.

Ward - an electoral subdivision of the City, headed by an Alderman. Two or more Common Councilmen are elected by the residents and businesses in each ward.

Ward Mote - a meeting of the ward's voters for the purpose of electing the Alderman or Councilmen for their ward.

Warden - a senior officer on the Court of a Livery Company. There are usually several grades of Warden who are on the path to becoming Master, Prime Warden or Upper Bailiff depending on the title of the most senior officer.

Yeoman - a term that some Livery Companies use to designate a Freeman of a Livery Company who is also a Freeman of the City of London. The word is not consistently applied across all Livery Companies. The word imports either sex.

Bibliography

Andersen, J. (2021). *An Introduction to the City of London*. Privately published.

Arnold, C. (2001). S*heep over London Bridge*. Corporation of London

Bromley, J.; Child, H. (1960). *The Armorial Bearings of the Guilds of London* (first edition). Frederick Warne

Clark, W. (2021). *The Lives of the Great and Good – Honorary Freemen of the City of London*. Phillimore

Clifford, H. (2018). *From Grossers to Grocers - The History of the Grocers' Company from foundation to 1798*. Paul Holberton Publishing

Corporation of London (Annual). *City of London Directory & Livery Companies Guide*. City Press Business Publishers (ceased publication in 2019)

Corporation of London (2011). *The City Livery Companies Brochure*. City Press

Ditchfield, P.H. (1926). *The Story of the City Companies*

Doolittle, I. (1982). *The City of London and its Livery Companies*. The Gavin Press

Greenglass, G.; Dinsdale, R. (2018) *Guildhall City of London*. Pen and Sword

Goddard, R. (2011). *Masters' Badges of the City of London Livery Companies*. Phillimore & Co

Goddard, R. (2017). *The Heraldry of the Livery Companies of the City of London*. Phillimore & Co

Gowman, A. (2019). *The City of London: Who, What, Why?: Plastering over the cracks in your knowledge*. Dowgate Press

Hall, M.; Hole, R. (2015). *The Honour and the Grandeur - Regalia, Gold and Silver at the Mansion House*. Paul Holberton publishing

Hatfield, E. (2015). L*ondon's Lord Mayors: 800 Years of Shaping the City*. Amberley Publishing

Hill, T. (2014). *Pageantry and Power: A Cultural History of the Early Modern Lord Mayor's Show*. Manchester University Press

Hope, V. (1989). *My Lord Mayor*. Weidenfeld & Nicolson

Hope, V.; Clive, B.; Gilbert, T. (1982). *The Freedom: Past and Present of the Livery, Guilds and City of London*. Barracuda Books

Jagger, P. (2018). City of London Secrets of the Square Mile. Pitkin.

Jagger, P; Cable, C. (2021). *Songs and Music of the City of London*. Privately published

Kenyon, N. (2012). *The City of London: A Companion Guide*. Thames & Hudson

Lang, J. (1975). *Pride without Prejudice*. Perpetua Press

Lubbock, P. (1981). *The Halls of the Livery Companies of the City of London*. Lavenham Press (based upon the original manuscript by W.A.D. Englefield)

Matthews, A.; Russell, H. (2018). *The Livery Halls of the City of London*. Merrell (photography by Andreas von Einsiedel)

Melling, J. K. (2008). *Discovering London's Guilds and Liveries* (Sixth edition). Shire Publications

Palfreyman, D. (2010). *London Livery Companies*. Oracle Publishing

Palmer, K. (1997). *Ceremonial Barges on the River Thames - A History of the Barges of the City of London Livery Companies and of the Crown*. Unicorn Press

Reid, D. (2015). *800 Years of The Lord Mayor's Show*. Third Millennium Publishing

Rules for the Conduct of Life. Oyez Press

Shand, W.; Wallington-Smith, A. *Heraldry & Stained Glass at Apothecaries' Hall*. (2020). PWP

Skinners' Company and Merchant Taylors' Company. (1984). *The Billesden Award*

Stuttard, J. (2008). *Whittington to World Financial Centre*. Phillimore & Co

Stuttard, J. (2023). *The City of London Sheriffs' Society*. Privately published

The Glaziers' Company (Undated). *The Outwith London Guilds of Great Britain*. M&B (Felsted) Ltd

Tucker, Tony (2006). *Visitor's Guide to City Churches*

Ward, H (1975), *Freemen in England*. Herald Printers (Westminster Press Ltd), York

Watson, B. (1993). *Airs and Graces*. Ashburnham

Whiteman, G (1970). *Halls and Treasures of the City Companies*. Ward Lock Ltd

Woolf, N.; Woolf, R.; Epps, A. (2015). *Lord Mayors' Portraits*. Art and Life Publications

'If you think that you understand the City of London, then you clearly don't understand the City of London'

- Daniel Boulet, 2014